A SPIRIT OF GOLF

Stories from Those Who Love the Game

Compiled and Edited
for The PGA of America
by John M. Capozzi

JMC Publishing Services
Fairfield, Connecticut

Copyright © 2001 by JMC Publishing Services
All rights reserved under International
and Pan-American Copyright Conventions.

Published in the United States by
JMC Publishing Services
A Division of JMC Industries, Inc.
125 Brett Lane
Fairfield, Connecticut 06430
(203) 255-8776

Library of Congress Cataloging-in-Publication Data

A SPIRIT OF GOLF: Stories from Those Who Love the Game
[Compiled and Edited for The PGA of America] by John M. Capozzi

First Edition

p.   cm.
ISBN 0-9656410-6-6
1. Sports & Recreation
2. History   3. Humor

Printed in Canada

A Spirit of Golf is dedicated to all of the members of
The PGA of America in recognition of their enormous contributions,
each day, to the game of golf.

INTRODUCTION

The PGA of America was founded in 1916 in New York City, with only 35 charter members. Since then it has become the world's largest working sports organization with more than 26,000 men and women professionals, and is credited with shaping the game of golf into the wonderful sport it is today.

While it is widely recognized that The PGA's regulatory and promotional efforts are directly responsible for the development of the game of golf as we know it, it is the members, the PGA Professionals, who have had the greatest impact on golf's increase in popularity. At every lesson and every tournament, we marvel at their skills, sportsmanship, and integrity. As you read through the stories in *A Spirit of Golf: Stories from Those Who Love the Game*, you will notice a common thread – no matter in what capacity they are serving; teacher, colleague, friend, the PGA Professionals' dedication of time and talent remains steadfast and contributes to the expansion of the sport and to the improvement of the golfing experience for all participants.

True to their very first objective, to "promote interest in the game of golf," PGA Professionals across the nation perform the small, everyday acts that make them true "heroes," not only to the game, but to the men, women and children they teach. Each PGA Professional is dedicated to enhancing the quality and integrity of the game. They make a difference every day.

A Spirit of Golf seeks to entertain, but also to broaden interest in the game of golf. Our mission is not only to inspire more people to play the game of golf, but to motivate golfers to take lessons as a way of increasing their enjoyment of the game. One of The PGA's founding beliefs is that golf education is universal, and should be shared with everyone.

A Spirit of Golf presents golf stories as varied as the "midnight lesson" given by PGA Professional Harry Pezzullo, to the ingenious construction of the "special club" designed by PGA Head Professional Jack Harden for Alan Shepard's famous moon shot. Readers will also enjoy stories featuring some celebrity golfers: Clint Eastwood, Jackie Gleason, Bill Gates, Tom Clancy, and Bruce McGill.

We have tried to profile many unique experiences of everyday golfers as well as those of PGA Professionals. We also highlight some examples of members going above and beyond the call of duty to help golfers improve and enjoy *their* game. *A Spirit of Golf* includes stories of Ben Hogan sharing his theory on practice, Johnny Williams coaxing shy 2½-year-old "Baby Jeffrey" to speak during their weekly lessons, members volunteering their time for the Special Olympics, and Warren Orlick spending his retirement years teaching golfers with disabilities.

The PGA of America also supports many initiatives for children. We are proud to identify that The PGA will donate 100 percent of the royalties from *A Spirit of Golf* to educational scholarship programs for children at-risk.

A Spirit of Golf is an interesting, humorous, and inspirational book that we hope you will enjoy. We are sure that you will find many stories to share with your family, friends, and colleagues (whether they play golf, or not!).

THE PGA OF AMERICA

The Professional Golfers' Association of America was founded Jan. 17, 1916, when a group of New York area golf professionals, accompanied by several prominent amateur golfers, attended a luncheon hosted by department store magnate Rodman Wanamaker at the Taplow Club in New York City. The purpose of the gathering was to discuss forming a national organization that would promote interest in the game of golf and help elevate the vocation of the golf professional.

Wanamaker, who viewed the public's growing enthusiasm for golf as the beginning of a national trend, promoted the idea of an association to help accelerate the growth of the game. Little did Wanamaker or his guests realize they were laying the groundwork for what would become the world's largest working sports organization.

Thirty-five charter members met and agreed to a constitution and by-laws on April 10, 1916, formally creating The Professional Golfers' Association of America. The Association's first order of business was to establish the organization's objectives. The members agreed to:

- Promote interest in the game of golf.
- Elevate the standards of the golf professional's vocation.
- Protect the mutual interest of its members.
- Hold meetings and tournaments for the benefit of members.
- Assist deserving unemployed members to obtain positions.
- Establish a benevolent relief fund for deserving members.
- And, accomplish any other objective, which may be determined by the Association from time to time.

After a decade in New York City, The PGA of America moved its headquarters to Chicago and continued to grow. In 1948, Dunedin (Fla.) Country Club became the first PGA National Golf Club. Dunedin also became the site of the PGA Merchandise Show.

From a humble origin in the parking lot of PGA National Golf Club, where salesmen worked out of the trunks of their automobiles, the PGA Merchandise Show expanded into large tents and steadily evolved into the world's largest golf exposition. The Show is today's world forum for the golf industry and makes its home in the massive Orange County Convention Center in Orlando, Fla.

In 1965, The PGA of America headquarters moved to the dynamic Florida East Coast and settled in its present home in Palm Beach Gardens.

When The PGA of America was formed, there was no distinction between club and touring professionals. Some of the greatest players in the game – Ben Hogan, Byron Nelson and Sam Snead – began their careers as club professionals.

As The PGA began to develop and promote tournaments, it became easier for touring professionals to devote their efforts to just playing tournaments and exhibitions.

In 1968, PGA tournament players, who comprised a small percentage of the membership, formed the Tournament Players Division and acquired more control of the tournament schedule.

By 1975, the Tournament Players Division was renamed The PGA Tour. Today, the PGA Tour is headquartered in Ponte Vedra Beach, Fla. The PGA Tour and The PGA of America maintain a close working relationship, and most professional golfers maintain dual memberships in the organizations.

As the Association enters the 21st century, The PGA of America is leading the growth of the game. That leadership takes root in many spheres. The PGA fosters a junior player's love and knowledge of golf and it develops instructional methods to bring enjoyment to the physically challenged. The Association also supports programs in the inner city that offer an alternative for underprivileged youth to build both self-esteem and golf fundamentals, and The PGA provides financial support for aspiring PGA Professionals.

The PGA of America, with more than 26,000 men and women professionals today, also conducts more than 30 tournaments for its members and apprentices.

The Association also proudly showcases its major spectator events – the PGA Championship, the Senior PGA Championship, the biennial Ryder Cup Matches – golf's most compelling event – and the season-ending PGA Grand Slam of Golf.

Through a network of 41 Section offices, the Association maintains a total commitment to the growth of the game and the development of the PGA Professional. The PGA Professional undergoes a rigorous training regimen of more than 600 hours and an average of 3^{1}/$_{2}$ years to be better prepared to meet the demands of today's marketplace.

The PGA of America's mission to grow the game is ongoing. The Association focuses on many vital issues that affect the game's future, such as pace of play, environmental concerns and accessibility.

Since its inception in 1916, The PGA of America has continued to establish standards of excellence for its members by expanding educational opportunities, programs and services. The Association continues to flourish following the principals set forth by its founders.

ACKNOWLEDGEMENTS

A Spirit of Golf: Stories from Those Who Love the Game, is the creation of many, and clearly, it would not exist were it not for the efforts of hundreds of contributors.

We wish to give thanks to all the members of The PGA of America and especially to the enthusiastic leadership team of The PGA of America. In particular, Jack Connelly, Joe Steranka, Jamie Roggero, and Julius Mason.

A special thanks to Bob Denney of The PGA of America for his dedication and energy in researching stories and communicating with PGA members.

An enormous thanks goes to Peter Smith of International Management Group for his friendship and guidance.

Clearly, a deep debt of gratitude goes to those industry publications who went out of their way to support The PGA of America and its members by providing an outreach to their readers which resulted in many of the fine stories that were submitted. Thank you to Keith Levitt and his colleagues at *Golf Digest* and *Golf World* for their unwavering support for The PGA of America, Rob Doster at *Athlon Sports* Magazine, Richard Summers at *The Majors of Golf* Magazine, Terry Russell and Michael Caruso at *Maximum Golf* Magazine, Jim Kuhe at *PubLinks Golfer* Magazine, and Fabio Freyre and Don Mahoney at *Sports Illustrated*.

Further, because The PGA of America has agreed to give 100% of its royalties to educational scholarship programs for disadvantaged children, we wish to also thank those publications that have agreed to assist The PGA of America in actually selling *A Spirit of Golf* to their readers. In particular, our special thanks to: Rob Doster at *Athlon Sports* Magazine, Jim Berrien at *Forbes* Magazine, Jack Haire at *FORTUNE* Magazine, Keith Levitt at *Golf Digest* and *Golf World*, Ernie Renzulli at *Golf* Magazine, David Brennan at *Golf Tips* Magazine, Richard Summers at *The Majors of Golf* Magazine and *PGA Magazine*, Terry Russell and Michael Caruso at *Maximum Golf* Magazine, Fred Stodolak at *Players* Magazine and The Golf Society of the U.S., Jim Kuhe at *PubLinks Golfer* Magazine, Fabio Freyre and Don Mahoney at *Sports Illustrated*, and Bob Weber at *Travel & Leisure Golf* Magazine. This assistance is invaluable to the success of *A Spirit of Golf*.

We thank the staff at JMC Publishing Services for their enormous efforts in researching, editing, and organizing the hundreds of stories that were submitted. In particular, Laura Cuddy, Michelle Stutzman, Annmarie Godwin and Marian Stone.

And, of course, thanks to all of the golfers and golf enthusiasts who submitted their stories to be included in this wonderful project.

Two-time Masters Champion Ben Crenshaw shared a special bond with legendary PGA Professional Harvey Penick (left) of Austin, Texas. Penick's inspirational lessons and words of wisdom extended beyond the playing arena. Penick was a source of strength and counsel for many Tour professionals and countless amateurs. His simple lessons of golf and life remain today some of the most respected perspectives on the game.

Harvey's Teaching

I think one of the best things about *A Spirit of Golf* is that it offers many of us who have spent a lifetime playing and teaching the game, the opportunity to share some personal observations with our readers. Hopefully, some of the advice you find will help you to enjoy the game even more than you do now.

I received some insight from Harvey Penick that has stayed with me for many years and I would like to share it. Harvey was a PGA Professional who had spent many years teaching the game of golf. He was asked to speak at a PGA seminar in Arizona. Harvey loved to speak to the PGA Professionals about his style of teaching and answer any questions they might have.

At the seminar, Harvey was asked a question from the audience regarding whether or not he believed in "group teaching." Harvey looked down for a moment and thought about his answer, "Well, I don't see how I could tell someone who slices and someone who hooks the same thing; so, no, I don't believe in group teaching."

Harvey believed in devoting time and attention to one person and one person only during a lesson. Each person needed to be worked with individually, so their specific problems could be diagnosed. This was the way Harvey taught golf. He always upheld the high standards of The PGA of America.

Ben Crenshaw
Winner of Two Major Championships
1999 U.S. Ryder Cup Captain
Austin, Texas

An Unlearned Lesson

As a 21-year-old assistant professional in my first season at Rolling Green Country Club, outside Chicago, I was eager to do a great job for my membership.

Among the first to take lessons with me was Mrs. Burton, an athletic woman in her mid-50s who played golf four times a week and routinely shot in the low 100s. After a few months of lessons, she was shooting in the low 90s.

Mr. Burton was a businessman whose dislike for golf was equally matched by his truly awful swing. Brad Burton played little golf, keeping his membership to pacify his wife's desire for the game.

In early June, the couple played as a twosome. After golf, I ran into Mrs. Burton in the clubhouse and asked her how the game went. She matter-of-factly replied, "Oh, I shot 124!"

"What?!" I asked, astonished at her nonchalant attitude.

"Don't worry," she snickered, "whenever I play with Brad, I have to shoot worse than he does or he'll never play again."

Three days later, I saw Mr. Burton having lunch and he called me to his table to inform me, "Listen, I'm getting a lot of charges for golf lessons for my wife, but I have to tell you – she's not getting any better!"

Peter Longo
PGA Life Member
Bensenville, Ill.

Be Concerned with the Important Issues

I was head professional at La Grande Country Club in Island City, Ore., for 18 years. As part of my routine, I usually played a round of golf with some of the members on Thursday mornings.

One morning, one of our club members came into the golf shop and mentioned that he wanted to try out a set of irons that he was thinking of buying. He was a good golfer with a low handicap, so I fitted him up with the irons and out we went to play. He did very well on the first, second, and third holes and commented that he would buy the clubs. However, on the fourth hole, he three-putted.

Unfortunately, on the fifth hole, another three putt. On the sixth hole, after another three putt, he completely lost his temper and threw his putter up into a big elm tree behind the green. It got stuck high up in the branches. He stood there just looking at it and then decided to climb up to retrieve it. As he stretched out to reach for the club, something occurred to me. I called out, "John, be careful! Don't fall! You haven't paid me for the clubs yet!" His reply was not in language fit for print. However, he did buy the irons and a new putter.

Ralph Moberry
PGA Life Member
La Grande, Ore.

Confidence When You Need It Most

I was competing in the 1980 Pensacola Open at Perdido Bay Country Club and was fortunate to be partnered with Chi Chi Rodriguez in the final round. We were in the middle of the pack, and we teed off early on the 10th tee because of inclement weather in the area. By using both the front nine and back nine tees at the same time, we were able to finish on Sunday.

It had been quite awhile since Chi Chi was in contention but he was off to a wonderful start with a 30 on the back nine and as we came around, he had a birdie on No. 1. There was quite a backup on the second tee, a very short par-5, and the delay gave Chi Chi time to realize that he was back in a significant tournament. With the ease of this hole and the way Chi Chi was playing, an eagle was a good possibility. Yet, I could sense a change in Chi Chi. He was taking more time and his usual chatter was missing. He backed away from his driver for the second time and then motioned for his longtime caddie, Sarge.

"Sarge, come over here and talk to me," he said.

I expected that he would ask Sarge a technical question, such as, "Should I go with a 3-wood?" But the hole was so wide open that I couldn't imagine what he was thinking. But Sarge knew.

As if on cue, Sarge began, "Cheech, you've got the best hands in the game. This hole is made for your game. I can see your ball starting down the right side and turning into the middle of the fairway. There is no one in the game better at this shot than you."

Finally, Chi Chi raised his hand as if to say, "That's enough." Sarge backed off and Chi Chi smoked one right down the pipe.

I often repeat this story to my students to illustrate how important confidence is, and that even the best players in the world struggle with self confidence. If the shot doesn't feel right, stop, back away, take a deep breath, picture exactly where the ball wants to go, and then re-address the ball with new confidence. Over the years I've come to realize that the difference between the great players and the rest of us is that they don't hit many shots without telling themselves they are going to hit a good one. They eliminate the negatives by replacing them with positive thoughts. And, in this case, if they are players like Chi Chi, who is having trouble putting positive thoughts in his head, they will rely upon someone else to help them.

Lonnie Nielsen
Director of Golf
Crag Burn Golf Club
East Aurora, N.Y.

A Special Fall

In the Fall of 1987, I went to play a recreational round at Bay Hill in Orlando, Fla. Prior to teeing off, I saw Arnold Palmer doing a clothing commercial for Sears on the practice range. Suddenly, he walked briskly toward me, smiled, and went into the clubhouse. Later that day, I made a hole-in-one on the 17th green with a 180-yard 5-iron. As I was heading to the parking lot to leave, there was Arnold putting his clubs in his golf car just 10 feet away.

No one was around, so I went over and told him about my hole-in-one. We talked for over five minutes about my ace, and The PGA, then he signed my scorecard and told me to, "Come back soon."

What was really amazing is that, a month later, he mailed a congratulatory letter to me at Winnetka Golf Club in Chicago, where I was working. I often wonder how many professionals, as busy as Arnold Palmer, would go out of their way to do something that special. Today, Arnold's letter and the scorecard he signed still hang on my wall.

Chris Anderson
PGA Professional
Charlotte, N.C.

A Mermaid on the Lesson Tee

I was blessed in two ways when it came to learning the game of golf. I was born of Italian ancestry, and in the early part of the 20th century, Italian-Americans distinguished themselves by their love of competition as well as teaching the game.

Secondly, I was born in East Rochester, N.Y., which is a hotbed of golf and a community that has produced many fine PGA Professionals including Walter Hagen, whose home was some nine minutes away.

I got to know Walter Hagen and enjoyed his style, his attire, and his love of people. At age 13, I began to caddie and learned to play reasonably well. As I grew older, I entered as many high profile tournaments as I could afford to enter. After World War II, I was named head professional in 1946 at Durand Eastman Golf Club, located on the northern side of Rochester on Lake Ontario. I enjoyed it so much that I stayed for 37 years.

One Sunday afternoon not long after the war, I was sitting in front of the golf shop when an attractive woman came up to me and asked about taking golf lessons. It was my policy to try to learn immediately about a prospective student's coordination, so I asked her, "Do you dance?" She said that she did, but added that she also was a swimming instructor. That immediately piqued my interest and I figured that if she was very athletic, I would not have that much of a problem teaching her to play golf. Also, I had never learned to swim, so I decided to make a deal with her. "I'll tell you what, if you teach me how to swim, then I will teach you how to play golf." She agreed to the trade of lessons and we moved to the practice range.

I was shocked at how good she was from the start. She stepped up, swung, and showed an immediate skill in hitting the ball. "If you teach me to swim as well as you appear ready to play golf, then we will be two pretty good instructors," I said.

The next day I made an appointment to go to the YWCA to take my first swimming lesson, but asked if I could go when nobody else was there. I did not want to panic in front of a crowd. I showed up for my lesson with tremendous anxiety and, when I got into the shallow end, she made me swim the width of the pool. That lesson ended and seemed to have gone well, until she added, "By your third lesson, you are going to swim the *length* of this pool." That did it. I panicked. The water has always frightened me. I nearly drowned once when I was 10 years old. Some neighborhood kids had thought they could teach me to swim by throwing me into a river and I never could handle deep water after that. Fear truly got the better of me, and I did not show up for swimming lessons again.

I always found some excuse not to come back. But, I really learned something from this experience about teaching. I learned that people need to have fun in order to learn – if they feel stress or panic, they don't have a chance.

What happened to the swimming beauty? Oh, she learned to play golf. The experience was not a total loss. I organized the first indoor group golf lessons at both the YWCA and YMCA.

Armand Lannutti
PGA Life Member
East Rochester, N.Y.

Tim Evans

Over the years, one of the most interesting things I have noticed about PGA Professionals is that they are very unique people both on and off the golf course. As a class, they seem to have a higher level of integrity than most. Perhaps it is because some of the basic foundations of the golf game are routed in honesty and integrity.

One such example is Tim Evans, whom I have known for many years. Tim is the head professional at the Deerfield Country Club in Boca Raton, Fla. He has a very demanding schedule managing the oversight of the facility, which he does with excellence. In addition, he has always been a very committed father, community leader, and an executive in the Boy Scouts in Boca Raton.

When his community was faced with the need for a new Scoutmaster, Tim was the clear choice. His involvement and commitment to excellence while supporting the local Boy Scouts has been exemplary over the years. He voluntarily accepted the role of Scoutmaster of Troop 333 in Boca Raton. This troop has over 60 boys actively involved in scouting. Tim personally contributed time and training to many of the boys to teach them the values of scouting, including giving the boys golf instruction to help them earn their golf merit badges. Because of Tim's professionalism and dedication to the sport of golf, many of his young scouts now want to follow his career path and become PGA Professionals.

Tim Evans is an excellent example of the high quality traits of a PGA Professional. For his business acumen, his personal values, his being a key role model for young men, and his ongoing support of the community and his Club ... Tim's career epitomizes *A Spirit of Golf.*

George D. Williams
Boca Raton, Fla.

A Great Lesson

Awhile ago, I played in a PGA Section event at the Long Island Montauk Downs. I was paired with Al Brosch, who actually won the tournament. One of Al's greatest strengths was that he could consistently strike the ball perfectly straight. Toward the end of the 36-hole final, I asked Al if he had any tips that could help me hit the ball as straight as he did.

He asked, "Sonny (I was younger then!), can you hit a fade?"

I answered, "Yes."

"Can you hit a hook?"

I again said, "Yes."

He replied, "Well, Sonny, don't do either!"

Joe Ennis
PGA Life Member
Jupiter, Fla.

A Bad Day on the Greens

In October of 1998, an executive from Salt Lake City, was playing golf at the Sierra La Verne Country Club in La Verne, Calif. He was wearing tennis shoes and they were slippery on the course. As he approached the fourth hole, his ball landed very close to a wire that was stretched between two trees to keep golf cars from crossing the fairways. He took out his 5-iron and, as he took his swing, he slipped on the wet grass. His golf club struck the wire, hooked the head of the club, and snapped it about mid-shaft. An 18-inch portion of the shaft, with the head still attached, then flew back off the wire and pierced right through the golfer like a sword.

The man calmly grabbed the head of his club, which was sticking out of the front of him, and walked back to the golf shop. I was in the golf shop when he came in holding the head of the club in his hand. He explained what had happened and, when we lifted his arm, we could see the blood and a part of the shaft protruding from his back. La Verne firefighters stabilized the man at our location and he was airlifted to St. Francis Medical Center, where his condition was determined not to be life threatening.

Golf is an amazing sport. Here is a golfer that sustained a serious injury and guess what this fellow asked us for? He asked that we return his club head so he could have it re-shafted. It certainly speaks well of him that he not only kept his composure, but also his sense of humor.

Dennis Troy
PGA Professional
Sierra La Verne Country Club
La Verne, Calif.

Doing the Right Thing

One thing we learn from Rule 18 is that when a ball at rest is moved by anything other than wind or water, it must be replaced. The question is whether it shall be replaced with or without a penalty.

During The 2000 PGA Club Professional Championship at Oak Tree Golf Club in Edmond, Okla., Steve Brady had a most unfortunate incident. Steve, who teaches golf at Oakland Hills Country Club in Bloomfield Hills, Mich., hit his second shot on the 18th hole near a fairway bunker about 50 yards from the green. Heavy Bermuda rough surrounded the bunker.

I was stationed about 100 yards from where Steve's ball had come to rest. As he walked near the bunker, he stopped and turned around, walked a short distance, and then called me over.

Steve said that he thought the ball was in the bunker and was not looking for it in the rough. When he walked by he stepped on it and it obviously moved. He was now unsure how to proceed. He knew that the ball moved when he stepped on it and he was well aware of Rule 18. So, even though the nearest witness was about 100 yards away, Steve dropped a new ball in the heavy rough and took a one-stroke penalty. The new lie was so bad that he could not play his next stroke to the green. The seven he made on this hole placed him one shot behind the last place to make The PGA Cup Matches Team. When Sunday's play was rained out, Steve lost his chance to make the team.

I talked to Steve during The PGA Championship at Valhalla Golf Club in Louisville, Ky., and I told him how proud I was of the way he handled a very difficult situation. Obviously, he was the only person who knew he had stepped on his ball and he called me to help with the ruling because he wanted to do the right thing. I must say that very few sports maintain a level of integrity as high as that found in golf. Clearly, professionals such as Steve Brady are the epitome of this integrity. Other sports could certainly learn a lot about character from golfers and their desire to play the game fairly.

Don Essig
PGA Master Professional
Indianapolis, Ind.

Ben Hogan, displaying his machine-like skills, during the peak of his career in the mid-1950s.

19 to 21 Hours of Golf ...

Shady Oaks Country Club, in Fort Worth, Texas, is the home of Ben Hogan. Having grown up in Northern Texas, going to the Colonial every year and knowing the history of the tournament and how special it was to Ben Hogan, I was still unprepared for what happened the day I passed my Players Ability Test.

Milling around in the golf shop after handing my card in, I watched, frozen, as Mr. Hogan walked in. While he walked around admiring memorabilia, every person who had played that day, except for me, was scrambling to buy mementos that he could sign. The most popular item was the famed 1-iron at Merion poster. I watched as he signed every poster that was brought to him and explained the shot that brought him the U.S. Open victory. Maybe it was fear, or intimidation, or the fact that I did not want to bother this member, but I never moved. He finished signing the posters and strolled out of the golf shop towards the Men's Grill.

Faced with the choice – either leave with only the memory of seeing Mr. Hogan, or buy two posters (one for me, and one for my father) – I bought two posters. I meandered my way through the club towards the Men's Grill, clutching the two posters in one hand and a black pen in the other, until I saw Mr. Hogan sitting at his table. He was stoic and silent as he looked out the window at the 18th hole, watching errant shot after errant shot miss their mark.

"Mr. Hogan," I stammered, "if it would not be too much trouble, would you mind signing these two posters for me?" He assured me that he didn't mind at all. Pointing to a spot on the poster at the bottom left of his perfectly balanced pose, he informed me that he always signed "right there." When I asked him to tell me about the famous shot, he told me to, "pull up that chair and sit down."

He did a lot of talking and I did a lot of listening. The conviction in his voice was powerful as he told me his theory on practice.

Practice was everything to him. He told me amusing anecdotes about his practice habits at night when he was traveling – how he would pitch balls into a pillow lying in a hotel chair. In regards to his late night practicing, he said, "My body is conditioned to only have three to five hours of sleep. That gives me about 19 to 21 hours to practice my golf."

He talked for about 30 minutes. It seemed like hours to me. I knew it was an opportunity that very few individuals had – to sit with Ben Hogan and talk about golf. More than that, I saw a side of this legend that not many people saw – his passion to share knowledge.

I often repeat Mr. Hogan's position on practice to my students – especially the ones who want to rapidly improve but can only practice a few times each month.

Barton D. Craig
Assistant Professional
Bent Tree Country Club
Dallas, Texas

Andy's Attention

A few years ago, I took my younger son, Parker, to the Westchester Classic. I am an avid golfer and was, obviously, very excited to attend. But Parker was only 9 years old at the time and was not yet into golf. He was just learning the game and his attention span also was not very long. I actually suggested that he bring some comic books with him, in the event that he got bored.

We found a lovely sunny spot, on a par-3, where we got settled – Parker with his comics and me with my program. We watched twosome after twosome go through and over time as anticipated, Parker started losing interest. I, on the other hand, could have stayed all day. To me, watching golf is probably one of the most relaxing and engaging experiences I know. I try to study the professional's posture, swing, and strategy, in an effort to improve my game. There came a time when my wonderful young son was anxious to leave, but I had not yet had enough.

Then Andy Bean came up to the fairway. As he approached the green, there was a positive reaction from the crowd. Parker put his comics aside and began to pay attention to Andy. At that moment, an amazing thing happened. Parker was staring directly at Andy and Andy took notice of Parker watching him. After putting out, Andy went out of his way to stop by and give Parker his golf ball. This was a huge event in Parker's golf life. He immediately felt special, as if he had been included in the tournament. I have often wanted to try to find Andy, to tell him that his simple gesture sparked Parker to become much more interested in the game.

Today, Parker plays most weekends with me and his brother at Wykagyl Country Club. The PGA professionals at Wykagyl – Mark, Charley, and Brian – watch us all wander the fairways as a family. Sometimes, when I am in the middle of a magnificent fairway on a beautiful day with my sons, I remember that one small moment, when a true professional, Andy Bean, personified what this game is all about.

Tom Gleason
Vice President
American Airlines
Darien, Conn.

Clint's Response

From 1994 through 1997, I was the director of instruction at the Carmel Valley Ranch Resort in Carmel, Calif. One of my more famous students was the actor Clint Eastwood.

Clint loves the game of golf, and even served as the chairman of the AT&T Pebble Beach Pro-Am. Today, he is part owner of the Pebble Beach Company, along with Arnold Palmer and Peter Ueberroth. Over the years, Clint played frequently, and he would periodically sign up with me to take a lesson.

One day during his lesson, we were working at the back of the range and Clint was struggling a bit. I would tell him what he was doing wrong and what he should do to fix the problem, but he was not getting it. After a few missed shots, I looked at Clint and with frustration in my voice, told him, "Clint, you really need to listen to what I'm telling you." With that, Clint stopped. He got that world famous "Dirty Harry" look on his face and, all of a sudden, all I could think about was, "Go ahead, make my day." He put his arm around my shoulder and said, "Shawn, I've got to tell you something. It's been a long time since I've had to listen to anybody." You really had to be there to understand the impact of what had just happened.

This was a very sobering moment for me. As it turned out, that interaction became a turning point in my life – it actually caused me to change the way I have coached students ever since. In an instant, I decided that my students would have more fun with the game. I also decided that stress (mine, or my students') was not worth it. Over the years, I have put more emphasis on "playing the game" and having fun, with less emphasis on intense coaching. My new philosophy actually broadened my relationship with Clint and he has become a much better player.

Shawn Humphries
Owner & Teaching Professional
SH Golf Inc.
Dallas, Texas

Dead or Alive

In the early 1960s, I was a member of Oak Cliff Country Club in Dallas, home of the then-Dallas Open and now Byron Nelson Classic.

The head professional, Earl Stewart, Jr., became, what I believe, was the only club professional to win a PGA-sanctioned event at his own course. Earl won the 1961 Dallas Open.

On the eve of the Dallas Open, as a means to inspire the volunteers, Earl had Mr. Nelson come over from Roanoke to give us a pep talk.

Earl introduced Mr. Nelson as, "The *only* PGA Professional living who has won 11 consecutive PGA tournaments."

Mr. Nelson acknowledged the introduction and added, "Earl, there's one small correction. I'm the only professional living *or dead* who has won 11 consecutive events."

Harvey E. Bradshaw
Grand Prairie, Texas

Conrad's Insights

In all of golf, I believe Conrad Rehling is one of the teaching professionals who has best used insight and humor as a learning tool for his students.

Conrad began his long coaching career at the University of Florida where he was golf coach for 22 years. After leaving Florida he coached for 17 years at the University of Alabama and then retired. In his "retirement," Conrad was instrumental in developing the Special Olympics Program for golf and he taught at the Golf Academy of the South for the next eight years.

Conrad has always managed to keep a healthy balance in his teaching, combining equal parts motivation, perseverance, and skill, with a big dose of humor. He developed his own special sayings to guide his students: "'GAS' stands for Grip, Arm and Swing ... when you run out of GAS you play like an a _ _," and he teased good-naturedly, "My players talk 68, they shoot 78, and they drive home doing 98."

Many of the young players that Conrad coached went on to achieve great success: Bob Murphy went on to win in the US Amateur; Tommy Aaron, who trained with Conrad, won the Masters; and Jerry Pate won the US Amateur and the US Open.

Part of Conrad's success as a teacher has come from his endearing personality and his great concern for others. He has always enjoyed working with young people and over the years, has dedicated hundreds of hours teaching golf to the physically and mentally disabled, always keeping frustrations in check, and the atmosphere light, with his distinctive wit.

In the world of golf, Conrad Rehling is a very special person.

Charlie King
PGA Teaching Professional
Tuscawilla Country Club
Winter Springs, Fla.

Confidence

A few years ago, I was playing a green surrounded by water. As I approached the ball, I recalled my teaching professional telling me that if I focus too much on "don't go in the water" all my body would hear is the word "water." I should have listened to him.

I focused so much on the "water" that I decided to hit a practice ball that floated – and sure enough, I hit the ball directly into the water. As luck would have it, the ball was floating near the edge, so I decided to save a stroke and attempt to hit it from its wet lie. I pulled out my wedge and struck the ball perfectly. Water went everywhere, and I was completely drenched, but the ball went right in the hole. Amazing!

However, now I listen to my professional. I do not even think about the water, I focus on the green. In fact, I even make a point of washing my ball at every water hazard knowing that I will not lose it. My professional taught me to have confidence and it works for me.

Thomas Smith
Westchester, N.Y.

Dave Stockton's Advice

Some time ago, I was playing in a tournament for the Los Angeles chapter of a worldwide organization of travel executives at the Riviera Country Club in California.

One of our members was a close friend of Dave Stockton and he arranged for Dave to come out and play several holes with each foursome. He eventually joined our group and, after watching me for two holes, he said, "George, if you don't stop hooding your clubs, you will never get real distance or accuracy!" His almost instant observation of my problem was a bit sobering. This was something I had been doing since I took up the game and his advice forced me to really address the issue. So, I started going to the practice range and working very hard to correct my problem. It was a hard habit to break, but I stayed with it and eventually conquered the problem.

I have gone on to play on every continent, in 25 countries, and on the "Old Course" seven times. But no matter where I play, Dave's advice is always with me. I think it is the single most important advice that I have ever received in my 54 years of golf. I thank Dave Stockton for being so quick to spot, and help me correct, my problem. He is what a golf professional is all about.

George Tibbetts
Salem, Ore.

Above and Beyond the Call of Duty

A few years ago, I left the Terry Walker Country Club in Leeds, Ala., around midnight after a party. About a half a mile away, while rounding a sharp curve, I lost control of the car and it flipped. I was dazed, upside down, and badly shaken, when another car stopped and a gentleman pulled me out of my car. I was bleeding from a good cut on my head, but since it was not life threatening, we decided to return to the club for treatment.

Our head professional, Billy Prentice, was the first to see me and was obviously shocked at my appearance. He took me to the locker room to get me cleaned up and evaluate my condition. The shirt I was wearing was my favorite Wilson Staff golf shirt that he had given me a few months earlier, and it was covered in blood. In my state of shock, the only thing I was worried about was that I had ruined my favorite shirt. After Billy had stopped the bleeding and cleaned me up, he called my wife to tell her that I was OK and then took me to the hospital to get my head stitched up.

When I got out of the emergency room at about 3:30 a.m., guess who was sitting in the waiting room comforting my wife? It was my PGA Professional with a new Wilson Staff golf shirt!

Billy Prentice is a wonderful person and a great example of how PGA Professionals go above and beyond the call of duty for their clients.

John Graham
Leeds, Ala.

Delivering Ben Hogan's Irons

In 1953, Ben Hogan was considered the best golfer in the world. That year, he won three major championships, as well as two other tour events. It was also in 1953, that Mr. Hogan became the first player to start his own golf club company.

In 1955, Ben was playing in the US Open at the Olympic Club, where he was hoping to win his fifth title. There were only two players at this event using Ben Hogan irons. The first was Ben Hogan, and the second was an obscure player from Davenport, Iowa, named Jack Fleck. Ben had personally delivered the Ben Hogan irons to Jack before the start of the championship.

Ben finished the final round and thought he had won when he heard that there was one player who had a chance to catch him. That player was none other than Jack Fleck. Jack birdied the 15th hole and then went on to birdie the 18th hole. This put Jack into a playoff with Ben, who was heavily favored to win. Jack Fleck played brilliantly to win the playoff before heading back to relative obscurity. The delicious irony is that Jack Fleck hit his Ben Hogan irons better than Ben Hogan did.

Peter Kessler
Golf Historian & Show Host
The Golf Channel
Orlando, Fla.

Arnold Palmer (right) relied upon the advice of his father, Deacon "Deke" Palmer, during his premier performance years in the game. Deacon Palmer started his son in golf when he was only 3 years old. Arnold's "Pap" also was an accomplished player despite having been stricken with polio as a youngster.

Arnie's Pap Was His Sole Guru

I am certainly not the only successful professional golfer who is also the son of a golf professional – but I may be one of very few who relied solely on his father's help during my best years. My dad, Deacon Palmer, started me in golf when I was only 3 years old. He showed me how to grip the little club that he had cut down for me and brought me up in the game at Latrobe Country Club some 50 miles east of Pittsburgh where he was the golf professional and course superintendent virtually all of his adult life.

By the time I was in high school, I was doing quite well with my golf around Western Pennsylvania. One day near the end of a match in a tournament in Pittsburgh, I missed a short putt and lost my temper. I sent that putter sailing over some nearby trees in my anger. Nonetheless, I won the match and the tournament, but got a very cool reception from Pap in the car on the ride back to Latrobe. Pap was angry with me. In no uncertain terms, he told me that if I ever threw another club like that, I would never play in another tournament. That was one of the many lessons of etiquette, good manners, and proper behavior on and off the golf course that I learned from my father. I never did that again.

Besides being an excellent teacher, Pap was a pretty good player in his own right despite having a bad leg, the result of having been stricken with polio as a youngster. One time in the 1970s, we came up with a format for a television show for NBC. I selected my "best" 18 holes in America and then played each of them with another professional or celebrity who was meaningful to that hole or course. It made a fine show, but, after we had finished a time consuming trek around the country filming the program, we decided to re-shoot one of the holes with a different player – the par-3 17th hole at my own Florida club, Bay Hill. I persuaded Pap to fill in.

The deal was, for the integrity of the show, the first shot counted. No mulligans. So what does Deacon Palmer, then nearly 70 years old, do in front of all those cameras but knock a 3-wood on the green of that long par-3 over water and run in a putt that must have been 40 feet long for a birdie two. I had to make my eight-footer to salvage a tie, but I think I was as happy about the whole thing as he certainly was. Playing with my dad was always a wonderful challenge to me and perhaps that is why playing in front of galleries never seemed to bother me.

Ironically, Pap died of a heart attack a couple of years later at Bay Hill a short time after playing 27 holes of golf on that very course.

Arnold Palmer
Winner of Seven Major Championships
1963, 1975 U.S. Ryder Cup Captain
Latrobe, Pa.

Meeting Lord Byron

In 1979, during my sophomore year at Abilene Christian University, I read a piece by Herbert Warren Wind on Byron Nelson. I had learned the game by starting as a caddie and I became captivated by Byron – a former caddie himself – both as a golfer and a gentleman.

When I finished reading, I set a personal goal: I would somehow meet Mr. Nelson, shake his hand and tell him how much I admired him. Of course, I had no idea as to how this would happen.

That summer, driving back to Abilene after playing in a tournament in Oklahoma, I took a wrong turn and I found myself driving on a two-lane state highway somewhere north of Fort Worth. I came upon a small town, Roanoke, and suddenly realized I was in Byron's backyard. Moments later, I passed some property bearing a sign "Nelson's Fairway Ranch" and slammed on the brakes.

This was it. This was the ranch where Mr. Nelson had begun his retirement while in his early 30s, still at the peak of his game.

My heart raced. As I drove over the cattle guard and up to his ranch house, which was back off the road surrounded by a grove of oak and hackberry trees, I could see the two-time Masters Champion sitting in his living room, looking out the bay window. As I got out of my Pontiac, he opened the front door and greeted me. I introduced myself, shook his hand and told him how, at that very moment, I was realizing one of my goals.

Mr. Nelson invited me in, but I told him I needed to get going, explaining how the wrong turn had thrown me off schedule. But he insisted, so we went inside, where Byron introduced me to his wife, Louise.

We visited for some 30 minutes, with Louise serving angel food cake and Coca-Colas, while Byron offered me advice on life and golf.

I thanked the Nelsons for their hospitality and drove back to Abilene in a semi-fog, unable to fathom just how fortunate I had been to have gotten lost. I mentioned as much in a "thank you" letter I wrote the Nelsons the following day.

When I wasn't attending class at Abilene Christian, I worked at Abilene Country Club in the bag room. When I told people at the club about stumbling upon Fairway Ranch and getting to meet the great man, several friends accused me of making up the story. One advised me to stop talking about it, because, he insisted, I was embarrassing myself.

Within days, though, I received a handwritten reply from Byron. When I flashed the letter around the clubhouse, one of the members offered to have it framed at no charge.

Byron Nelson visited Abilene that semester to conduct a fund-raiser for the ACU golf team. It turned out that he was, and is, a big supporter of Abilene Christian University. His brother, Charles Nelson, was on the ACU music faculty for many years.

Byron and I got reacquainted that day, and after he conducted a clinic for about 70 people, he asked me to ride several holes with him and hit some shots. I was so nervous with him watching that I could barely take the clubhead back.

In the ensuing two decades, Byron and I have visited on several occasions, exchanged letters, and attended the same church services.

I've also paid a couple more visits to Fairway Ranch and become acquainted with Peggy Nelson, whom Byron married a few years after he lost Louise.

As a symbol of the respect and admiration I have for Byron, my wife, Mona, and I christened our son, born in 1992, Dylan Byron Connell. If my son lives up to the standards of humility and grace set by his namesake, he'll be quite a gentleman and I'll be a proud father. Byron inspired my career in golf with his grace, humility and by a simple comment to "do it the right way."

Not long ago, at the wedding reception for a mutual friend, Byron told me that Tony Lema, the 1964 British Open Champion, had driven back and forth in front of Fairway Ranch three times before he could muster enough nerve to cross the cattle guard.

I had made it to Byron's front door on my first attempt. My sense of direction may have been mediocre, but I've never been bashful. Taking the wrong road on my way home from Oklahoma is one of the best mistakes I've ever made.

Courtney Connell
Director of Golf
Fair Oaks (Texas) Ranch Golf & Country Club

How to Plan a Fire Sale

I turned professional at age 24, and ultimately became the head professional at Green Hills Country Club in Muncie, Ind. During that time, I was fortunate to have two gentlemen who served as my mentors: Dr. William Deutsch and Mr. Rhode Shannon, chairman of the golf committee. I served for 23 years at Green Hills and I believe these two gentlemen had more influence on me than anyone else in helping me to understand people and to advance in the golf business.

One memory I'll never forget occurred in my early years at Green Hills. At that time it was common to dispose of old boxes and other refuse by burning it in used oil drums. Early one evening, I started burning refuse in a drum on the edge of the club property. Unfortunately, it was the same time that a dance was being held in the clubhouse and the wind turned. As the smoke started drifting in the direction of the clubhouse, Dr. Deutsch came out and was furious with me. He said that I was spoiling the dance.

A day later, we ran into each other and he apologized to me. I assured him that future garbage fires would not occur when events were happening at the clubhouse.

Not long after that, I noticed that I had five or six of the same style ladies hats on display in the golf shop and wanted to mark them down for our Ladies Day golfers. So, I put up a sign next to the hats that read "Fire Sale."

A few ladies who had attended the dance wandered into the golf shop to look over the inventory. With a smile one of them said loudly, "We shouldn't buy a hat now. Let's wait until our professional moves them to the oil drums for his real Fire Sale."

Don Padgett
PGA Past President
Executive Vice President & Director of Golf
Pinehurst (N.C.) Resort & Country Club

On Second Thought

One day, Gary Parker, the PGA Professional at Tumwater Valley Golf and Country Club in Washington, was working the counter at the golf shop and a customer who identified himself as a "new golfer" came in to rent clubs.

The customer was so new to the game that he did not even know if he needed left- or right-handed clubs. Upon receiving his clubs, the customer spotted the price for range balls on the wall and ordered a small bucket. Gary, thinking he was off to the practice range, provided him with his range balls and then told him to be on the first tee in about 30 minutes.

The customer left but immediately returned and said, "Maybe you'd better give me a large bucket of balls ... I am not sure I can get around the course with only a small bucket."

Joe Robertson
Shelton, Wash.

The Golf Swing Needs Rhythm

I grew up in St. Paul, Minn., and played golf from 1947 to 1949 at the University of Minnesota where I was fortunate to have Les Bolstad as my coach. Les not only improved my golf game when I played with the university's Golden Gophers, but before he would retire in 1976, he would often coach against me when I was named head golf coach in 1958 at the University of Iowa.

Les provided exceptional golf assistance to his university students, as well as to golfers from across the country. Top tour players such as Patty Berg and Beverly Hanson were just a few of his past students. And, even Babe Zaharias came in at times for some pointers.

I learned so much from Les that has allowed me to help others throughout my career. He was always quick to give you a tip, whether you were ready for it or not. One of the most valuable tips he gave me came one day at a meet. I was at the range hitting a bag of practice balls when he sauntered over to observe. "Chuck, you're swinging awfully quick," he said. "You've got to remember that rhythm is a critical element in a golf swing and your rhythm should be one-and-two, not 12." I've used that tip with my students ever since.

Charles "Chuck" Zwiener
PGA Life Member
Former University of Iowa Head Coach
Iowa City, Iowa

Guiding a Great White Shark

When I graduated from Aspley High School in 1972, my life had no clear direction. Against the better wishes of my parents, I decided a career as a professional golfer would be the path I would follow. Because of that decision, my path crossed that of a PGA Professional who would eventually leave an indelible mark on my career and in the end, my entire life.

In 1974 my family joined the Royal Queensland Golf Club where Charlie Earp was the head professional. Eventually, Charlie gave me a job in the Royal Queensland shop in 1975 and paid me $38 a week. The requirements set forth by the Australian PGA were much different in the early 1970s than they are now, and for that matter, much different than they have ever been with The PGA of America. In order to become a touring professional, regardless of your amateur record or potential, you first had to complete your requirements to the Australian PGA as a trainee professional, gaining a thorough grounding in all facets of the game from a business perspective. In the United States and Europe, and now in Australia too, you can become a touring professional without spending time as an apprentice.

Charlie was very generous with my schedule, allowing me to work mornings and have the afternoons off – as long as I spent my time off practicing. Aside from my time on the practice fairway and in the shop, I devoted much of my time to bookwork in hopes that I could complete my trainee requirements ahead of schedule, which The PGA of Queensland and The PGA of Australia allowed me to do.

Charlie was always there, pushing me to stay motivated with my studies and also helping me with my game. He became my mentor, a man that to this day I trust and count among my closest friends. Charlie didn't take his obligation as boss lightly to those who served under him in the golf shop. He ran a tight ship, and as long as I worked hard I maintained my practice privileges. I soon learned that regardless of your potential, if Charlie believed any of his assistants were not working hard enough – he had a saying, "There's the door, what's the hurry?" – and a promising golf career would come to an end. I respected Charlie's authority and learned as much as I could from his teachings.

It wasn't until years later though that I really began to appreciate the time I spent behind the counter at Royal Queensland. Today, as I continue to play professionally as well as develop businesses, I credit Charlie with much of my success. Everything I learned as an apprentice – making clubs from a block of wood, merchandising, inventory control, club repair, etc. – has been extremely valuable, especially now that I own an equipment distribution business in Australia. While I didn't quite understand at the time why I needed to learn all these business-related activities, looking back, it was an invaluable experience.

My time with Charlie has led me to become a huge supporter of the programs offered by The PGA of Australia, The PGA of America and other associations like them. I'm such a supporter of The PGA that I have chosen to give something back by acquiring the Australian PGA Championship and bringing that Championship back to a level of prominence it once enjoyed and richly deserves. Ultimately, I have Charlie to thank for giving me the ability to help.

Greg Norman
Winner of Two Major Championships
Hobe Sound, Fla.

Making a Difference

Every once in awhile, I receive a letter about a PGA Professional that epitomizes what our profession is all about. Not long ago, Mr. Randall S. Paa of New Ulm, Minn., wrote me about his 16-year-old daughter, Amanda. He told me how much she has grown in character, self-confidence, and ability as a direct result of the training she received from Mike Luckraft, the head professional at St. James Country Club in Minnesota.

Amanda struggled with swing problems and after achieving a 97 score at her high school conference met with Mike only six days before the qualifying event for her state tournament. Mike agreed to help Amanda and starting at 6:30 a.m. the next morning they embarked on a daily training program that enabled her to qualify for her first state AA tournament.

Rather than abandon her at that stage, Mike attended the state tournament and worked with Amanda on the practice range after her first round.

With Mike's help, Amanda continued to improve and when she played in her first USGA Jr. Girls Sectional Qualifier, Mike even made time in his schedule to caddie for her. This enabled him to help coach her through the round and to deal with the stress of tournament competition. It also helped him identify additional areas in her game that needed improvement.

Amanda continues to improve and her dad said in his letter: "PGA Professionals like Mike Luckraft are rarely recognized for the difference they make in peoples lives. Mike's work ethic, professionalism, character and dedication to the game have made a huge impact on our daughter … both in her golf and in her personal life.

Our family is proud to know Mike Luckraft. He truly exemplifies the title of PGA Professional."

Mike Tracy
President
Minnesota PGA Board of Directors
Stillwater, Minn.

All Square

One of the reasons golf is such a great game is that it is totally unpredictable. The combination of luck, skill, and pure fate is very unique to this sport.

One day I was playing with my friend, Dave, who regularly shot in the mid-80s. I was a scratch golfer so, to make the round a bit more interesting, I decided to give him 10 shots on the nine holes. On the ninth hole my friend had played so well that he'd only used three of those shots. We were standing on a 384-yard dogleg with me having to make up seven strokes. I hit my drive across the tree line, which was a short cut, and landed on the fairway less than 100 yards from the slightly elevated green. Believe it or not, Dave hit his drive into the woods on the left. His third shot found the water in the middle of the fairway. His fifth shot came up short. He knocked his sixth shot over the green and in the meantime I knocked my sand-wedge within a few feet of the pin.

Dave's seventh shot was on the green and he 3-putted for a 10. I made my putt for a birdie. We walked off the green that day all-square. Golf ... you just never know!

Willie E. Jackson
Milwaukee, Wis.

Building a Business the Old Fashioned Way

Back in the early days when we were building the TaylorMade Golf Company (1981), Gary Adams and I agreed that to be successful in the marketplace, our clubs had to have acceptance on the PGA Tour. This was a real challenge for us.

We decided that it was time to come out with a really hot fairway wood that looked and played like a spoon, so we designed the "Tour Spoon," which had a real strong loft of 13 degrees and a low center of gravity. We felt that we had a winner, but only if we could get a meaningful amount of Touring Professionals playing it.

We had 13 of these little honeys and it was the week before the Andy Williams San Diego Open, so I said to Gary, "Let me take these babies out there and see if I can get some of the professionals to try them." I had played on the Tour for 12 years and knew many of the top professionals personally. Gary said, "Go for it!"

I hopped on a plane and before you know it, I was on the practice tee at Torrey Pines with some of the greatest players in the world. Miller Barber was hitting balls next to Andy Bean and a new rookie by the name of Paul Azinger was also there. I waited until Miller started to practice with his fairway wood and then I slipped up with my bag of Tour Spoons. Miller and I were rabbits together, so I felt I had a pretty good chance of getting him to try the "Tour Spoon" because of our past association. When I un-holstered the club to show him, he said, "What have you got now, Langert? A practice range club you want me to hit? Get out of here."

I said, "Hey, Miller, you and I go all the way back to our college days and I told Gary Adams that I knew a bunch of you guys personally and that you'd try our new 'Tour Spoon.' So won't you please hit just *one* ball with it, so I can tell Gary that you hit the club?" I looked up at Andy and Paul, who were now watching, and said, "Maybe you guys will help me out, too?"

Miller sighed and said, "OK, give me the club and I'll hit one for you, Langert." In those days we didn't have range balls like they do today, but caddies with our own personal shag balls. Miller's caddie was standing where he had been hitting spoons to him and when Miller let the first one fly with the "Tour Spoon," it went 30 feet in the air right over his head and easily carried 20 yards further. That was about it. It wasn't long until Andy and Paul were burning them out there and that just created a happening on the tee line. The rest of the day became unadulterated fun. Within two days I had all 13 sold and I believe nine were used that week in the tournament.

Eddie Langert
PGA Life Member
Carlsbad, Calif.

Perfect Form

My daughter, Kathy, joined a beginner golf class at the Washington Athletic Club in Seattle. She was one of eight girls, most of whom had never held a golf club before. One of the points the instructor repeatedly drilled into the students' heads was holding the position with the club in the air just before swinging. He explained that you should have your left arm straight across your body and your right arm at a 90-degree angle, "The way a waitress would hold a tray."

The instructor soon made the assumption that Kathy had received some instruction in the past and repeatedly pointed out to the others in the class what a great swing she had, to the extent that the other girls in the class started ribbing her. Kathy began to feel a little self-conscious and felt obligated to confess to some of the girls that her dad was a golf professional and that he had worked with her on the practice range and that they had played golf together.

As the end of the sessions approached, the instructor videotaped all the girls taking a swing. The class watched each student's tape as the instructor made some final brief comments. When Kathy's segment was played he paused the tape frame-by-frame commenting on her set-up, her position, her stance, and on and on. When he paused on the frame where Kathy had her club raised in the air and her right arm was in a perfect 90-degree angle, he told all the students to pay special attention to how perfectly it appeared as though she was holding a tray. Finally, an exasperated student exclaimed, "Yeah, but her father is a golf professional!" and another piped up, "... and her mother is a waitress!"

Larry Brown
Head Professional
David L. Baker Golf Course
Fountain Valley, Calif.

Jim Furyk competes in the historic 1999 Ryder Cup Matches at The Country Club
in Brookline, Mass.

Best Advice Not Given

I have been a golf professional for the past nine years and estimate that I have given at least 2,000 lessons. I would like to believe that I have given some good advice to my students over the years and have been able to improve their golf games. However, I think my best advice was the advice I chose to *not* give to Jim Furyk back when we were in high school competing against each other.

The situation occurred when our high school golf team hosted a match against his team. Jim was a member of one of the best high school teams in the state and was ranked among the best junior golfers in the nation. His reputation was well-known throughout the county and the state.

Our high school golf team, on the other hand, was in its first year of existence. To make matters worse, I was a relatively new golfer barely breaking 100 and I was the best on our team – the team captain. Needless to say, we were not favored in this match even though we were playing on our home course.

Every player on our team was eager to see this renowned player despite the fact that we suspected we were in for a crushing defeat. There was no practice range to warm up on so, right after they arrived, our teams headed directly to the first tee. Jim was the first to hit and he hit the ball further than any shot I had ever seen up to that point. The ball seemed to stay in the air forever. He nearly drove the 320-yard first hole. And lucky me, I got to follow him. Reaching into my vinyl bag with my used set of mix-and-match clubs, (the whole thing, including the bag, cost less than $150), I pulled out my trusty persimmon driver. Undaunted by my opponent's monstrous tee shot, I calmly countered his shot with my own "powder fade" as I liked to call it. My ball ended up about 80 yards behind his, slightly more to the right, and in tall grass.

However, to my credit, we each proceeded to knock our second shots onto the green, my ball stopping on the other side of the green from where the hole was located. Jim's second shot nestled 10 feet from the pin. I was the first to putt. Despite my high average, I was a decent putter. So, I lagged my first putt close enough to the hole to tap it in – a great start for me.

What I saw next absolutely astonished me. Jim was taking a few practice strokes on the fringe of the green while the other players in our group took their turns on the green. Jim played golf right-handed, yet here he was with his left hand lower on the putter grip than his right hand. Maybe he putts left-handed, I thought. When it was his turn to putt, he replaced his ball on the green and lined up the putt from both sides of the hole. When he returned to his ball, he addressed it from the right-hand side and took the same left-hand low grip on the putter.

Could it possibly be? Here was this future PGA Tour star lining up his first putt of the day and he did not even know how to hold the putter correctly. I was shocked. Should I say something before he putts? Jim put a nice smooth stroke on the ball and it found its way to the bottom of the hole for a birdie. I decided not to correct him because he must have been lucky on the first one. Besides, I couldn't. That would be giving advice and I would be penalized two strokes.

Jim putted very well that afternoon, despite using the wrong grip. I elected *not* to give him any advice on his unorthodox putting style.

Looking back, it is a good thing I did *not* give Jim my advice that afternoon. Jim has gone on to be a star of the PGA Tour and actually led the Tour in putting one year.

The great thing about teaching is that you continue to learn the more you teach. I eventually learned what "cross-handed" putting is. I have also learned that sometimes the best advice you can give is no advice at all.

Jamie Komancheck
Assistant Professional
Aronimink Golf Club
Newtown Square, Pa.

Bad Boy Turned Good

In 1971, I was an 18-year-old college freshman just hoping to get hired by the new professional in town. I was sure that I was going to be hired as I had worked in the golf shop (actually it was a little broken-down, one-room building, nothing more than a starter shack), for three years. When I finally had the chance to meet Mr. Hogan I knew that I had to make a good first impression, so I cut my hair. That was hard because in 1971, long hair was cool. Luckily, he hired me, and I had the good fortune to work for Terry Hogan throughout my college years. Terry even helped me decide on a major.

My only real desire was to make money, play golf, and flirt with women. It amazed me how many second chances Terry gave me in the four years I worked for him. He gave me the nickname "Late Clayt" and kept me on after finding me on the course in a golf car after it was closed due to rain. He knew better when I called in to say that I was not able to come in to work because my car broke down (when actually, I was partying on the other side of the state). He even forgave me when I took a pretty young lady into the golf shop during a wedding reception in the clubhouse – I was trying to impress her – and set the security alarm off. The cops showed up with their guns drawn.

I kept asking Terry when I could become an assistant professional and he kept putting me off, saying that I had to work in the business full-time.

When I graduated from St. Cloud State, I declared to Terry, "Now I'm ready for my own job." Terry just happened to be the employment chairman for the section that year and I ended up interviewing for head professional jobs in every little farming community all over the state. With Terry's help, I was offered a job in Fergus Falls. What an eye-opener! It was a great experience and I met my wife, Sandy, there. We've been married for 24 years.

The long and short of it is, Terry Hogan taught me that an important part of being a PGA Professional is customer relations. I marveled at how he could sweep the walk while chatting with the guys from Federal Cartridge one day, and the next day play a round of golf with the president of the bank. Terry was considerate and sincerely interested in everyone that he came into contact with. I was very fortunate to have had Terry Hogan as my mentor. Every club should be as fortunate to have a professional with Terry's skill with people.

Mike Clayton
PGA Master Professional
University Park, Fla.

A Cy Young Winner By My Side

Each year, one of my goals is to qualify for the Bell South Classic held in Atlanta. In April of 1998, I went to the Country Club of the South for a practice round. When I arrived, I told the golf shop that I would be happy to play with anyone; juniors, ladies, or whomever. One of the golf professionals looked at the tee sheet and said, "I believe that we will pair you up with Mr. Maddux." I said, "That will be great, I just want to get a feel for the course in preparation for the qualifier."

The starter called us to the tee. Mr. Maddux came over to me and introduced himself. I said, "It is a pleasure to meet you, Mr. Maddux." We loaded up on a golf car and proceeded to play 18 holes.

On one shot, I assisted him when he landed in a cavernous green side bunker and had given it a couple of strokes, but was unable to advance the ball on to the green. I told him to open the blade of his sand wedge, move the ball forward, and to keep the blade pointed to the sky on his follow through. The ball came out nicely and landed two feet from the hole. Mr. Maddux just shook his head when he saw the results. Later, the professional asked me how our game had gone and I answered, "Great! I gave Mr. Maddux a few pointers … I think he has potential."

I thanked the professional for allowing me to play with Mr. Greg Maddux, the five-time Cy Young Award winner. I guess he has great potential. I will remember that four hours forever.

Michael Thomas
PGA Professional
Sugar Hill, Ga.

Never Quit!

In March of 1997, as a PGA Club Professional, I qualified to play in the Doral Ryder Open in Miami. With my brother as my caddie we had a late Friday tee time. Unfortunately, darkness came and we were unable to finish our second round ... with only three holes left to play. I had played well, but it was clear that I was not going to make the cut because I was a few too many over the projected cut number. I should have told an official that I was going to withdraw, but I knew I could not because I represented our local PGA Professionals and I wanted to properly finish for them.

So, on Saturday morning, I arrived at the course and went to the practice range to warm up. I turned around and saw a man walking up to the range ... it was my dad! Now with just three holes left to play I asked myself, why would dad come all this way to watch me finish the last three holes? Dad simply said, "I know you could have withdrawn last night and I am proud that you did not. I came down to watch you finish your Doral Ryder Open."

Well, I went out to the seventh hole and teed off, I made par. I played the eighth hole and also made par. I got to the ninth, a 176-yard par-3. It was my last hole in the tournament. I could see my dad in the distance, he always walks ahead of the group, and he was sitting on the bleachers around the green. The pin was back to the left. With a little wind in my face, I addressed the ball and made myself feel very comfortable. I blanked out my dad, my brother, and the other spectators, relaxed, took a deep breath, and made a great swing. I looked up and saw that the ball had good alignment and when it landed it took two hops and rolled right into the cup. What a thrill! The first hole-in-one in my life, and at a PGA Tour event, the Doral Ryder Open. Even more important, my dad and brother were there to see it.

Dad had always taught us never to give up or quit. He felt that someday I would benefit from my hard work and dedication. Understanding the circumstances for completing the round made this a special moment and I am thankful to have shared that with my family.

For a moment, I stood frozen with tears in my eyes. I was so glad I had not quit the night before … for my PGA colleagues, for myself, and for my dad who always taught my brother and me to never give up. At that moment I could not have been prouder to be a PGA Professional.

John Nelson
PGA Professional
Coral Springs, Fla.

Nine in Time

In 1997, at the Albemarle Plantation in Hertford, N.C., I was fitting one of my members for a new set of irons. At that time, I was using the Titleist fitting system. Well, we went through the whole thing and decided on the head style, the lie angle, shaft type, shaft flex, and grip size. Now, it was time to decide on the set makeup. When I asked the member what clubs he wanted, he said he wanted the 3-, 4-, 5-, 6-, 7-, 8- irons, the pitching wedge and the sand wedge. I noticed he did not say he wanted the 9-iron, but I thought it was just an oversight.

When I questioned him about it, he said he did not want the 9-iron because he had shanked a 9-iron in a tournament in 1963 and had never hit one since. Well, I thought more than 30 years was a long time to hold a grudge against a golf club so I convinced him to get the 9-iron to at least help his resale value. I would be willing to guess, however, that if you looked in that fellow's bag right now, the 9-iron would look like new.

Jim Nodurft
PGA Professional
Hertford, N.C.

Official on the Green

Sometimes, when the pressure is on, you just need to keep a good sense of humor. At the 1980 PGA Championship, I was assigned to the 13th green as a Rules Official. Hubert Green had just taken a shot when one of the marshals called me over as Hubert's ball had come to rest against the leg of his cane stool. I told the marshal to stay where he was and Mr. Green would handle the situation. Evidently, Hubert did not hear my statement because he challenged me as to why a Rules Official was involved. I explained to him that the marshal had called me. With that, he then loudly informed me that he did not need an official looking over his shoulder as he had, "Served his time and paid his dues." Before he had completed his dissertation, my face was as red as the jacket I was wearing. I could not get away from him without walking on the green or through a bunker.

Before playing his stroke, Hubert sarcastically asked me if I wanted to play the shot. With a smile, I told him I was a Rules Official because I could not hit a shot like that. He proceeded to skull the ball over the green, and then told me that maybe he should get a red jacket and become a Rules Official. With a laugh, I told him that he would not be able to handle that, either. We both smiled and went our separate ways.

James R. Carpenter
PGA Past President
Timberton Golf Club
Hattiesburg, Miss.

Divot Controller

I started working as the controller at Bulle Rock Country Club in the fall of 1998. I brought with me a lot of management and accounting experience – but definitely not in the golf industry. In fact, I knew nothing about golf when I started. Being enthusiastic about my new job and trying to help "control" costs, I studied various invoices for possible unnecessary or excessive expenses and one day was sure I had found a way to save a lot of money.

We had received an invoice for 100 "divot repair tools." I researched this vendor and found that we had bought many of these divot repair tools over time. So, with the invoices in hand, I proudly and confidently marched into the golf shop to talk to our professional. I told him that I was sure that if we purchased "better divots" from the start, we would not need to buy so many divot repair tools! I could not understand his immediate look of disbelief followed by some serious laughter by all the golf shop staff.

I have learned a lot since that embarrassing day two years ago, but what is really important is that our golf professional has gone out of his way to help me ... he is a professional both on the course and in the office.

Barbara Aselage
Bulle Rock Country Club
Havre de Grace, Md.

Once a Golfer ...

I literally have grown up and spent my entire career in the golf industry. My dad was a PGA Professional, my twin brother, Dick, is a PGA Professional and I am a PGA Professional.

My dad spent 43 years at the Texarkana Country Club as the head professional before retiring in 1977. He replaced his good friend, Byron Nelson, who was leaving for the PGA Tour. Dad was 91 years old and lived alone. Even though he was 91, he was still quite fit and played golf three or four times a week. However, given the realities of his advancing age, my brother and I decided we should consider finding him an assisted living home to move into.

We flew down to Dad's home on the border of Arkansas and Texas to visit with him. The temperature was over 100 degrees when we arrived. The first thing he asked was, "You guys want to play golf?" We explained to him that we wanted to look at some assisted living places. Dad wasn't pleased. "I don't want to do that! I want to play golf." We again explained our plan. Finally, Dad agreed to go with us and we all drove out to a really nice looking place.

As we waited in the reception area for the admissions person, a nice elderly lady came by and said, "Hello" to some other folks she knew in the lobby and turned to Dad and asked him if he was a new resident.

Dad said, "No, I'm just out here with my boys. They're getting older and are looking for a place to stay."

We all had quite a laugh over that and then the admissions person arrived. Dad threw her a bit of a curve when he asked if the home had cable. She told him it did. He then asked if they had The Golf Channel. Only when she told him, "Yes" did he agree to look around.

Dan Murphy
PGA Professional
Dunwoody, Ga.

Snap Shot

Not long ago, I was playing with my professional at Bulle Rock Country Club in Havre de Grace, Md.

On the 11th hole I hit my 4-wood from the fairway and it shanked directly at my partner. I yelled, "Fore!" as the ball flew directly at him. It hit the shaft of his 4-wood and shattered his graphite shaft.

Before I could apologize, he laughed and said that he had wanted to replace the shaft anyway. It was an amazing shot ... but my professional's forgiving attitude was even more amazing.

Lance Murray
Belair, Md.

Bill Strausbaugh (left), one of the most influential PGA Professionals of his time, dedicated his career to improvement in employment conditions for his fellow professionals. His work inspired the creation of The PGA's Career Services Department.

We Called Him "Coach"

I have never met a golf professional, or a person, quite like Bill Strausbaugh. He was one of the most uniquely gifted people one could ever meet and it was my pleasure to know him. Bill was the head golf professional at the Columbia Country Club, outside of Washington D.C., for what seemed like an eternity.

We called him "Coach," and when I first met him I was a PGM intern from Ferris State University, working at TPC Avenel, across town. I had heard his name mentioned from time to time around the campus at Ferris because of the influence he had in bringing the first PGA-sanctioned golf management program to this Northern Michigan college.

We went over to play one October day because the season was ending and Columbia was slowing down for the year. It was a chance to get out on one of the finest courses in the East. My foursome was comprised of other Ferris PGMs, and when we walked into the shop we were introduced to Mr. Strausbaugh by his assistant, Jon.

"Boys, my name is Bill Strausbaugh. What are your names?" I was the first to speak up and I blurted out, "Sean, Sean Mulligan." He looked me right in the eye, with a stare that was warm, but serious, and repeated my name. "Sean Mulligan … Sean Mulligan … Sean, it's good to meet you!" He then repeated this with the others and said as we left for the first tee, "Fellas, it's our pleasure to have you as our guests. Enjoy the course and if you need anything at the snack bar, tell them to put it on my account."

We were amazed at his manner of greeting, the ability of this great professional to take a minute to meet us, and how he treated us as if we were dear friends. It really seemed like he wanted to know our names – why else had he repeated them so many times?

A few years later, I was visiting TPC Avenel during the Kemper Open and I made my way over to the practice tee. I spotted a familiar face inside the ropes talking to Fred Couples. "Isn't that Bill Strausbaugh?" I said to my friend, Scott. "Yeah, it is ... and here he comes." He happened to be walking in our direction and, as he got closer, he noticed me standing there. He paused, looked at me again with that warm stare, and said, "Sean Mulligan. How are you?" I nearly fell over. I could not believe that he remembered me – I had only met him once. I laughed as I said, "I'm doing great ... uh, how are you?" "I'm doing fine," he said. "I'm just here to talk with a few of my friends." He stood there and spoke with us for 10 minutes about the swings of the players we were watching warm up and we watched other players go past and say hello to him. He was an encyclopedia of information about the golf swing. After we said goodbye and left, I felt again like that first day in his shop ... like a friend.

It was later that I learned that The PGA had recognized the accomplishments of this man by naming a national award after him, the Club Relations award, (for outstanding service to The PGA in improving relations with golf facilities), and by naming him PGA Teacher of the Year. He helped Jim Flick write a book in the '70s called, *Square to Square*. He had written countless articles for *Golf Digest* and *Golf* magazine. He had done everything that a PGA member could aspire to achieve – and yet, he had the time and the humility to speak to, and encourage, aspiring golf professionals, like myself, and others, all over the country.

But what I really wanted to know was, how *did* he remember my name?

Three years later, I was attending the Teaching and Coaching Summit at the Superdome in New Orleans. While I was waiting for a friend on the concourse surrounding the field, with hundreds of people passing by, I suddenly noticed "Coach" making a beeline for me. "Sean Mulligan!" he shouted, "How are you?" I was again stunned that he recognized me and, as he had each time before, made a point to stop and say, "Hello." "I'm doing great, Coach," I said. "How about you? How is Columbia Country Club?" "Well Sean, I'm changing gears," he said. "I'm going to retire at the end of the season." "Good for you," I said. "A chance to rest a little."

"No, no, no, Sean. I'm changing gears ... I'm not stopping!" He rushed off, after saying goodbye, to learn more about the golf swing, even though he could be considered one of the most well-versed PGA Professionals in the game.

Another three years passed. I was at the Westchester Country Club for the Buick Classic with my wife, Laura. I spotted "Coach" from a distance and pointed him out to Laura, who had heard me speak about him often. I told her that he might mention "changing gears" and that we would all laugh. We walked over and I tapped him on the shoulder. He turned around, paused, and then said, "Sean Mulligan, how are you, my old friend?" "I'm doing great, but Coach, I want you to meet someone. This is my wife, Laura."

I couldn't help but smile at his next words: "Laura Mulligan ... Laura Mulligan ... Laura ... it's a pleasure to meet you, Laura. You know, your husband and I have known each other for quite a while."

"He has told me a lot about you, Coach. Are you still changing gears?" Laura asked him.

"Oh yes, Laura," he said with a smile, "I have a lot to keep me busy. There is so much I still have to learn about this game!"

After a few minutes, we said goodbye, not knowing it would be our last conversation. The next year he became ill and after a long struggle, passed away. He left behind so much, though – so many people touched by his warm, gentle ways; so many golfers who had become better players because of his efforts; so many PGA Professionals who carried on his passion for always seeking more; so many friends who found that his heart was his most pronounced feature.

I am always impressed and bewildered when I think of Bill Strausburgh. I remember him often … especially when I meet new people and I watch the expression in their eyes as I repeat their name.

Sean P. Mulligan
Head Professional
The Links at Shirley
Shirley, N.Y.

It's How Many

As the golf coach at the University of North Carolina-Wilmington, I often scouted the area for potential young golfers for our golf team. On one afternoon, I happened to be playing golf with a young man when we approached a par-3 hole. The young golfer watched as I sailed my 7-iron shot onto the green. He asked what club I had played and I replied, "Don't worry about the number, just use the club you feel most comfortable playing. Remember, it's not how, it's how many." I happened to look at the club he was using, which was a 4-iron, and thought I had made a mistake with my suggestion. The boy stepped up, took a practice swing, and then struck his shot toward the flag.

With one bounce the ball hopped into the hole for a hole-in-one. Ed keeps in touch and reminds me from time to time, that it's not the how, but how many!

Greg Stenzel
Director of Golf
Raleigh (N.C.) Country Club

Damaged Goods

A few years ago, I was the head professional at Fairview Golf Course near Lebanon, Pa. Our golf car staging area consisted of a blacktop section of pavement with a grid pattern painted to show where the golf cars should be lined up. This grid did not allow for much room between golf cars and forced members of a foursome to be quite close together while staging to go to the first tee.

It was shortly before 7:30 a.m. and I was returning from the first tee to the golf shop when I noticed that one member of the next foursome had moved in front of the line of golf cars and was taking practice swings with an iron. The first two swings stayed successfully above the blacktop. The third, full-speed swing, came crashing to the ground in a noisy display of sparks and flying blacktop pieces.

With the close proximity of his fellow players, as well as a few other foursomes, a loud barrage of laughter quickly ensued. The gentleman's riding partner, an older man, was making the loudest display, falling to the ground with laughter, pointing, and almost choking while holding his stomach. Then suddenly, he stopped. It seemed that the gentleman swinging the club had decided to swing one of his partner's new King Cobra clubs to warm up. The club had never hit a golf ball and now, by looking at the bottom of the club, it was difficult to even tell what iron it was.

As the head professional, I ran over and offered to repair the club immediately, but the group decided to continue on. After several minutes of apologizing, offering to buy a new club, and even more intense laughter by everyone else within sight of the occurrence, the group reluctantly moved to the first tee.

After the round, I fully expected to receive the club so that it could be replaced, but to my surprise, the club never came in. Apparently, the owner had holed his second shot on the third hole, a 430-yard, par-4 and the number 1 handicap hole, with the beat-up 4-iron. This was his first, and to the best of anyone's knowledge, his only eagle. He never did replace the 4-iron.

John W. Zesiger
PGA Professional
Lewistown (Pa.) Country Club

Desert Dream

As the son of a PGA Professional, I grew up on golf courses. I not only learned to play the game, but I was also taught how to maintain a golf course.

In the early 1960s, I became a member of The PGA and at that time, my future career choices in golf were: teacher, merchandiser, player, or management. The management aspect seemed very interesting to me and I began studying golf course management. I fulfilled the requirements for the classification of a "Master" PGA Professional and went to work for a golf course construction company in Southern California. I built three golf courses for this company and at the last one, I became general manager and had the opportunity to set up the entire operation.

One day I was at an exhibition at a trade show and met a man from Saudi Arabia who was looking for a person to come to Saudi Arabia and build a golf course. This man was seeking someone who was a golf professional, golf course superintendent, and had experience in building golf courses. Obviously, these are credentials that not too many people possess. Throughout my early career, I had always dreamed of traveling to foreign countries and now, after 35 years, my dream was about to come true. There were a lot of people interested in the opportunity, but I was offered the job and in 1993, I moved to Saudi Arabia.

My first year in Saudi Arabia was somewhat difficult. The culture is very different, the climate is unique (hot), and not everyone speaks English! But I acclimated and spent most of my time planning my golf course development strategy.

The area where the course was to be built was a desert, barren of any greenery – total sand. I made trips to the Philippines and India to recruit workers who had to be trained in every aspect of building golf courses in difficult locations. My Filipino supervisor knew how to grow grass and take care of it in hot environments and we built a magnificent nine-hole golf course, a clubhouse, and other necessary facilities. Not only did we design the course itself, but we created a very involved irrigation system, planted grass everywhere, and put in more than 2,500 trees. Today, there are more than 15,000 trees planted on the property.

In the first year after we opened the course, we were not making a good return on the owner's investment. I realized that in the lackadaisical attitude that is prevalent in this environment, I had lost the ability to get things done the way I was taught. I now needed to bring myself back to the management techniques that had brought me to my job in the first place. So, in our second year, we established new systems and controls and today, we are a financially successful operation. We have also gone on and designed and built the second nine holes.

Since leaving America, I have had the opportunity to play golf in 15 different countries, and because of my PGA membership status, I have been treated like a dignitary in all of them. Further, I have found that the most respected golf professionals in the world are American. The education and training that is required by The PGA of America for membership in our Association is the best in the world. The salary for American PGA Professionals is higher than any other nationalities as well.

Being a PGA member has been the fulfillment of a lifetime dream. Now that I am living that dream in Saudi Arabia, I plan to stay here until I retire.

Jim Christie
PGA Master Professional
Dirab Golf & Recreation Center
Saudi Arabia

It's All About Job Security

One day, I looked over at the practice range and saw some guy hitting golf balls while wearing blue jeans. I mentioned to one of my staff that we run a first rate golf and country club with quality members so, "Go out there and tell this guy that our club does not allow jeans on the range."

My assistant went outside and proceeded to tell Bill Gates to go home and change into more appropriate attire.

The good news is that Bill took it in good spirits, went home, and changed his clothes. The better news is that he did not buy the club and fire me.

Ron Hoetmer
Head Professional
Overlake Golf and Country Club
Bellevue, Wash.

By the Way, Where's Bob?

In 1975, while working as an assistant professional at the Dallas Country Club, an amusing incident occurred which I will never forget.

The membership at this club was very senior and many of our golfers were well into their 80s. One day a foursome of seniors reached the par-3 16th hole which played over a serious water hazard. One of the fellows hit his drive into the ravine and decided to try and retrieve the ball while his partners continued playing the hole. The older gentleman got down the bank with no problem, but could not get back up the steep incline. The other three seniors finished the hole, not realizing that their partner was missing. After playing the 17th and 18th holes by themselves, they put their clubs away, changed their shoes in the locker room, then the threesome sat down for a drink in the men's grill. It was then, they realized Bob was missing from their usual gin game. They headed back to the golf shop where they enlisted the other assistant professional, Corky, and me to help find their lost buddy.

After reviewing the facts, we headed back to the 16th hole and, sure enough, found the forlorn golfer still struggling to climb out of the ravine. After fishing him out, we returned a weary but all right golfer back to his foursome.

I have come to realize that each day as a PGA Professional brings new and different challenges. This little incident was only one in the line of duty.

Greg Befera
Head Professional
Baraboo (Wis.) Country Club

Personal Professional

As a member at the Charles River Country Club in Newton, Mass., our club professional Andy Froude did me a favor in 1995 that I will never forget.

On August 11th I was playing golf at the club with three of my friends. I had a great front nine, making three birdies and shooting 33. As an 8 handicap, I was pretty excited that I had a career round going. As we finished the ninth hole the assistant professional suddenly approached us and told my friend that he had to call home right away. Apparently his son had fallen and hit his head and had been rushed to the hospital. We were all concerned and a bit shaken by the news. My friend insisted we continue our round, but with only three in our group, we decided to call it a day. As we were leaving the golf shop and preparing to go home, our professional Andy Froude heard me say that I had shot a 33 on the front but was calling it a day because of the situation. It was a busy Friday at the club and the golf shop was totally full of people, but Andy looked at me and knowing how excited I was about my round, he suddenly said he would make arrangements to find coverage at the golf shop so he could join our group and play the backside with us. My career round since joining the club in 1983 was 75, and Andy knew this was my chance to break 70.

When we got to the 10th tee, I was still very shaken over my friend's son being injured, but Andy totally calmed me down. He focused on the little things, like to relax and not let my grip pressure get too tight. I birdied on the 10th, and parred the 11th, and 12th holes. When I got to the 13th hole my ball landed in a divot, but Andy again told me to relax and take the shot. I sculled it and made a 6 – but with Andy's help I recovered. I birdied the 16th hole and on the 18th hole, I made a 10-foot par putt for a 69.

I thank Andy Froude, my PGA Professional, for taking time on a busy day to give me the support and calm advice I needed to post a "career" sub-70 round and give me a memory I will never forget. I still have the card and soon it will be mounted with a picture of the 18th hole – my last birdie. I salute Andy – his actions epitomize *A Spirit of Golf.*

Neil Abbott
Boston, Mass.

Chandler Harper of Portsmouth, Va., was a club professional when he captured the 1950 PGA Championship at Scioto Country Club in Columbus, Ohio. Harper later became a premier instructor, who had as one of his many students, a major champion – Curtis Strange.

Buttercup on the Course

I was the golf professional at the Bide-A-Wee Golf Club in Portsmouth, Va., and operated the club for 37 years. During that time, I thought I had seen just about everything a PGA Professional could see at the club. But, one day I truly saw it all.

I was in the golf shop chatting with one of our club members known by his nickname, "Buttercup," when another member, who was having an awful day, came in. This member had a notorious temper and was known to break multiple clubs every time he played. After today's difficult round, the member was clearly frustrated and announced that he wanted to give his clubs away. "Buttercup" who was standing nearby, immediately said, "I'll take them."

The member turned to him and said, "Good, they're yours!" I thought, what a wonderful gift, but then he continued, "There's a half dozen balls in the pocket along with some tees, ball markers, and a few divot repair tools." I did not think the offer could get any better, but it sure did. He then said, "… and there's a brand new sweater in the side pocket. You can have that, too!"

With that, I was totally unprepared for what happened next. "Buttercup" looked at the member and inquired, "No umbrella?"

Chandler Harper
1950 PGA Champion
Portsmouth, Va.

Drinks in the Dark

I think my story represents what *A Spirit of Golf* is all about –
golf professionals on and off the course.

It was the first week in November 1965, and while I was attending
a meeting in New York City, the entire city experienced a total
loss of electrical power. We were left totally in the dark. My
wife and I were staying at the Essex House Hotel and our only
option was to walk up the darkened stairway to our room on the
19th floor.

As we stopped on the 5th floor landing exhausted, a man came up
the stairway carrying a bucket of ice and a candle. It was Arnold
Palmer. We exchanged "Hellos" and continued the climb to the
19th floor. Really exhausted, my wife and I were about to say,
"Goodnight" when Arnold insisted that we come to his room for
some food and drinks. We agreed, and sat by candlelight, talking
about golf into the wee hours of the morning.

My family owns a restaurant called "Pals" in West Orange, N.J.,
near where Arnold had a distributing plant for his golf clubs.
The plant manager was a client and a week after the blackout he
came into the restaurant and said, "I hear you met The Boss." He
presented me with an autographed picture of Arnold inscribed,
"To Marty, remember the blackout, good luck with your golf."
He also said that Arnold would like me to come to the plant and
pick out a set of clubs, which I did. I still have the clubs and still
use the putter, which is an "Arnold Palmer Personal" model.

I have met Arnold Palmer on several occasions since that night in
New York, and he always remembers the blackout. I do not think
too many super celebrities would have done what he did on that

very scary night ... but then, he is a professional golfer. I guess that explains it.

Martin L. Horn, Jr.
Hobe Sound, Fla.

Heroes

When I was 12 years old, Ted Fox, the professional at Tryon Country Club in North Carolina, gave me my first pair of golf shoes. They were his old shoes but were still in great shape. The only problem was I wore a size 6 then and the shoes were a 10!

These were "Ted Fox's shoes" and I was so proud of them that I stuffed the toes with paper to make them fit so I could wear them to my Pro-Junior Tournament.

Ted Fox was a professional who made a difference in my life. He was a hero to me and I am sure his positive influence encouraged me to go on to also become a golf professional. Today, I pass along all of my old golf shoes to disadvantaged kids and I hope I will have the same positive influence on them that Ted Fox had on me.

Chris Burns
Head Professional
Florence (Ala.) Golf & Country Club

First Tee Shot

In the summer of 1981, as my foursome was walking to the first tee at the Athens Country Club in Athens, Ga., Terri Moody, who was then the NCAA women's golf champion from the University of Georgia, came up and asked me if she and her male partner, (whom we did not know), could tee off in front of us and then quickly move out of our way. I obviously, said, "Yes," in part due to the fact that Terri was not only as cute as a bug, but she was also a good friend, a great golfer, and a former student of mine at the University.

Her partner teed his ball and promptly hit it off the toe of his club into the top of a tall pine tree to the right of the tee. My immediate thought was that this guy was a real hacker, and now he was ahead of us and we would be forever finishing our round. Terri's face turned as red as a beet and she told her friend to take a mulligan. So, her friend teed another ball and split the middle of the fairway with a 300-yard plus drive. My entire foursome just stood there stunned by this amazing drive until Terri introduced us to Hal Sutton, the then National Amateur Champion. He was a friend of Terri's and had come to Athens to visit her.

Since that day, I no longer worry about taking a mulligan on my first tee shot.

Frank R. Bowers
Athens, Ga.

For Better or Worse

My father was a tremendous baseball player. Everyone always spoke of his baseball talent. As hard as I tried, I could never achieve his level of skill. I certainly enjoyed Little League, but I was only an average player.

One day I had a particularly terrible game. I struck out four times. Following the game, as I walked to the car dragging my feet and crying, my dad asked, "What's the matter, pal?" "Nothing …" I replied. "I can tell something's bothering you, Mason. Now why don't you tell me what it is?" he said. I looked up and said, "I'll never be as good as you. You were such a great baseball player. And I love the game so much. But I'll never be as good as you were, Dad. Never."

There was a slight pause and then my dad said, "That's right. You'll either be better, or you'll be worse." As it turned out, those were words I'd never forget.

Years passed, and I discovered golf. I took to the game of golf like my father took to baseball. I worked very hard and became good at golf – much better than I was at baseball. I continued working and eventually became a professional.

One summer afternoon, my father and I played a round of golf together. Upon completion, on our walk to the clubhouse, my father started rubbing his face with both hands and shaking his head. He had managed to play particularly poorly that afternoon and was obviously frustrated. On the other hand, I had played quite well that day. "What's wrong, Dad?" I asked. "Nothing, pal." he said. "No, Dad, I can tell something's not right. What are you thinking about?" I persisted. "Well, Mason, you make it look so easy out there. Your swing is so simple and you hit the ball so well. It's fun to watch, but at the same time, it is also somewhat frustrating, because I know that I will never play like that, no matter how hard I try."

Before he finished speaking, I already knew what I was going to say. We both smiled as I spoke. "That's right, Dad. You'll either do better, or you'll do worse."

Mason Champion
PGA Professional
Baltimore, Md.

From the Mouths of Babes

At Woodfield Country Club in Boca Raton, I am in charge of the Junior Golf Program. Teaching young children the game of golf can be pretty amusing, as I learned one day after giving a 5-year-old his first golf lesson. As his mother took his hand to lead him away, she looked down at him and asked him, "Camden, what do you say to Mr. Williams?" Expecting a polite, "Thank you," I was tickled when the youngster turned and gave me a thumbs-up sign and said, "Johnny, you're the best!"

I really enjoy seeing my kids gain confidence in their golf swing and I went out of my way to coax a few words out of one of my less talkative students. I was giving lessons once a week to a 4-year-old girl, named Megan, who picked up the game pretty well and developed a nice swing in just a couple of lessons. Her mother would often bring Megan's 2½-year-old brother, "Baby Jeffrey," to watch. The toddler would hit golf balls next to his sister with a plastic golf club and would cry when he was told he had to stop and go home. One day, towards the end of Megan's lesson, she began to get tired so I started helping Jeffrey for the remainder of the half-hour, using Megan's lightweight kids' clubs. It was probably my third lesson with "Baby Jeffrey" when I noticed he never said a word during our lessons, only nodding yes or no. Midway through our fourth lesson, Jeffrey swung and the clubhead hit the ground about six inches behind the ball and bounced over it for a whiff. Determined to engage him in a bit of conversation I said, "Jeffrey, we call that a 'boo-boo.'" No reaction. I teed up another ball for him and he swung and ripped it about 20 yards towards the first target green on the practice range. Then, the usually silent young man looked up at me and said, "That's no boo-boo!" I laughed and teed up another ball. On his next shot, this 2½-year-old took his club back and squarely struck the ball, sending it straight down the range about 25 yards. It was an amazing thing to watch and to my delight, Jeffrey looked up at me and said, "That's what Tiger Woods do."

Johnny Williams
Assistant Professional
Woodfield Country Club
Boca Raton, Fla.

Gleason's Water Walk

A number of years ago, when I was a young assistant golf professional at Shawnee-On-the-Delaware in Pennsylvania, I had the privilege of playing a round with the then-owner and bandleader, Fred Waring, and the famous comedian Jackie Gleason. During this time, construction was underway for nine additional holes and Mr. Waring had the final say about the design of the new course.

On the fifth hole, a par-5, Jackie Gleason sliced his drive into a dirt-covered area being excavated for a future pond. Since this area was a "pond" it was marked off as a "water hazard" rather than "ground under repair." When Gleason stepped over the rope and walked into the area to play his ball, Fred Waring complained, "C'mon Jack, what are you doing? That's a water hazard!" Gleason looked at Waring and very apologetically replied, "I'm sorry Fred." He then walked out of the area leaving his ball in place.

After exiting the area, Gleason then rolled up his pant legs to his knees and did an outrageously funny tippy-toe walk back to his ball and played the shot safely out. Fred Waring quite sarcastically replied, "Very funny, Jack!" I thought it was one of the most comical and spontaneous acts I have ever seen on a golf course.

Vince Yanovitch
Director of Golf
Great Bear Golf & Country Club
Shawnee-On-Delaware, Pa.

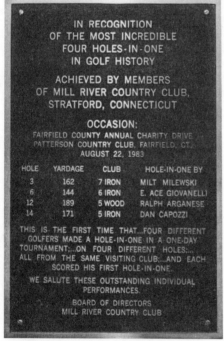

A foursome of star-crossed golfers gather at nearby Patterson Country Club in Fairfield, Conn., the site of their historic golfing adventure of Aug. 22, 1983. On that day (from left: Dan Capozzi, Ace Giovanelli, Ralph Arganese and Milt Milewski) all recorded their first career holes-in-one. The four were all members of nearby Mill River Country Club of Stratford, Conn. A plaque at Mill River Country Club today honors the foursome. It was the first time that four different golfers made a hole-in-one in a one-day tournament on four different holes.

The Day Came Up Aces

On Aug. 22, 1983, the Patterson Country Club in Fairfield, Conn., hosted the Fairfield County Annual Charity Drive. Milt Milewski, E. Ace Giovanelli, Ralph Arganese, and Dan Capozzi, four golfers from nearby Mill River Country Club in Stratford, Conn., arrived for the event, none of them knowing that they would make history on that day.

On the par-3 third hole, Milt Milewski pulled out his 7-iron and teed off. His ball soared 162 yards, rolled across the green, and dropped into the hole, giving him his first hole-in-one.

A little later that day, E. Ace Giovanelli stepped up to the par-3 sixth hole to tee off. He swung his 6-iron and his ball sailed 144 yards. It hit the green, bounced once, and rolled right into the cup! Even more intriguing – it was his first hole-in-one.

Ralph Arganese chose his 5-wood to tee off at the par-3 12th hole. With a textbook swing, his ball flew 189 yards to the green – and landed right in the hole. Another "first" hole-in-one.

Dan Capozzi, having now heard about his three colleagues amazing day, stepped up to the par-3 14th hole with his 5-iron. He connected squarely with the ball, sending it 171 yards down the fairway. It rolled up on the green and went right into the hole, giving Dan *his* first hole-in-one.

That day marked the first time that four different golfers made a hole-in-one in a one-day tournament, on four different holes. The fact that all four golfers were from the same club, and that it was the first hole-in-one for each golfer, made the feat even more amazing.

We placed a beautiful bronze plaque on the wall in our club grill room to commemorate the event, but as the head professional at Mill River, I only wish I had a dollar for every time I have heard this story told around the club.

Fred G. Kolakowski
PGA Professional
Mill River Country Club
Stratford, Conn.

Golf Clubs Reincarnated

Back in the late 1980s, I was the head professional at the Las Colinas Sports Club, home of the GTE Byron Nelson Classic. During my tenure there, I developed a special relationship with Byron. I used to cherish the days that Byron would visit our golf shop and use my office and desk to sign autographs. It was fascinating to hear his stories about the old PGA Tour and all of his triumphs and teachings.

One day, a member brought in an old set of MacGregors and said they had been given to him by a friend who said that they were originally used by Byron Nelson. He was hoping to have them authenticated by Byron and see what he could sell them for. My original thought was that he was kidding because the clubs were awful, completely covered with rust – they just looked terrible. But, I humored him and told him that I would have Mr. Nelson take a look.

Within a few days, Byron came in to sign his autographs and I reluctantly pulled out the old clubs to show him. Byron immediately recognized the clubs, saying they were the set he used to win the 1955 French Open. The clubs were specially designed for his international trip to the British and French Opens. I was flabbergasted! I could not believe these nasty looking clubs could ever have done anything so spectacular.

We sent them to Golfsmith to have them refurbished and they came back looking like one of the most beautiful sets of clubs I had ever seen. A specially designed copper insert had been shined on each club and the head was crisp and detailed. They were awesome! The member who brought the clubs in was also totally taken aback by their beauty and graciously donated them to Byron to be displayed.

Byron had me create a shadow box and mount them in his Trophy Room at the club – they were a great addition. Later that year, the USGA had a special exhibit honoring Byron at the Golf House where the clubs were featured in the showcase. They still hang on the wall in Byron's Trophy Room at the Las Colinas Sports Club in Irving, Texas, if you are ever in the area.

David Kaspar
Head Professional
Lake Charles (La.) Country Club

Great Open

Last summer, as the coach of our high school golf team, I had the opportunity to take one of my students to the Greater Milwaukee Open. He brought along his younger brother, Lucas, who is confined to a wheelchair due to the symptoms of Multiple Sclerosis. At the tournament, Casey Martin, Steve Stricker, Corey Pavin, Jim Gallagher, Grant Waite, Fuzzy Zoeller, and several other professionals spotted Lucas. I was so proud of these professionals who took the time, during a professional golf event, to go out of their way to make sure that Lucas enjoyed his day.

All the attention, autographed balls, and plenty of signatures on Lucas' cap were the highlight of the day for this young man. They made Lucas really feel a special love for the game. The *Milwaukee Journal* ran a human interest story on our visit complete with a picture of Casey Martin giving Lucas special attention on the ninth green after he putted out for a birdie.

Lucas now wants to play on my golf team. I have offered him the chance to become our team's official statistician when he gets to high school. The day was a wonderful experience for my wife and I, and especially for Lucas. To say these professionals are GOOD is not even close to how great they are.

Pat Hauswald
Friendship, Wis.

Double Eagles

I am the head professional at Overbrook Golf Club in Bryn Mawr, Pa., a position that I have held for the past 10 years. I have been a golf professional for 18 years, and as a member of the 1986 PGA Tour, two time PGA Cup Team member, and five time participant in the PGA Championship, I have been fortunate to have seen first hand many great golf accomplishments.

This year was a celebrated year at Overbrook Golf Club. It marked the club's 100th Anniversary and the opening of the newly renovated clubhouse. But, one of the most incredible feats of this year happened on the golf course.

It all started on a sunny afternoon in August during our monthly Scotch Foursomes event on the 313-yard, par-4, 14th hole. The Curtins, who are members at our club, had both taken golf lessons from me. John Curtin, a golfer with a 34 handicap, stepped to the tee and hit his Orlimar 5-wood to about 95 yards from the green. He then proceeded to hit his second shot with a wedge. The ball flew over a pond in front of the green and went right in the hole for an eagle 2. It was an amazing shot.

However, even more amazing, a month later John was playing in the first round of our annual President's Cup mixed tournament with his wife, Sarah. She hit her drive on the 14th hole approximately 105 yards from the green. Then, John once again took out his pitching wedge and proceeded to hit his next shot right in the hole for another eagle 2. Here is a member with a 34 handicap with two eagles on the same hole. Hopefully, everyone will attribute this success to his great golf instructor! That second eagle ended up helping get the Curtins into a playoff, which they eventually won, to win the 2000 President's Cup. Lessons are vital for the success of any golfer and I honestly believe the lessons and instruction helped the Curtins to accomplish their victory.

We have all heard about great golf happenings, like holes-in-one and double eagles, but to me, this is one of the most incredible feats I have personally witnessed in this great game of golf.

Stu Ingraham
PGA Professional
Overbrook Golf Club
Bryn Mawr, Pa.

Growing Up with Golf

As teenagers, young men are very impressionable. Many summers ago, I spent my days at a local country club in the 100-degree weather beneath the Florida sun. Watching and working with the golf professionals at my club had a great influence on me. Dreams of being on a PGA Tour weaved their way in and out of my mind. With the help of my club professional, a patient and skillful instructor, my handicap slowly trickled down to 18 … 15 … 13. While my improvement was steady, it was certainly not good enough to allow me to turn professional after high school graduation – my plans were ruined.

The summer before my senior year, golf was my outlet. As I walked those same nine holes I thought about life. Things became so clear to me as I trudged along those endless fairways. While my friends were out doing usual teenage things, I was on the golf course.

Golf taught me a lot about life: it is not fair, it is very inconsistent, and it brings about tremendous amounts of fury, followed by surges of jubilation. You can never predict how things are going to turn out – you play each shot where it lies, and make the best out of what is given to you. I applied what I learned on the golf course to everyday life and found it to be very helpful. Aside from being the greatest game ever created by man, golf is a learning tool. Golf is a trek through obstacles, and requires immediate decisions and learning to keep your head straight. Teenagers are impressionable, but there is nothing that has made an impression on my life more than growing up with golf.

Chris Harrison
Tallahassee, Fla.

I Just Aimed and Hit It There!

It was just another sparkling June morning in Maine with the sun rising on the 18th fairway, when PGA Professional Dick Harris beckoned me over. "Hey, Bill, I need you to go down and give a lesson!" he called.

I was told a "baseball celebrity" was filming a commercial and had asked for a 15-minute lesson during his break. When I reached the set, I was immediately cornered by the star who demanded, "I want to know what you teach and how you can help me get rid of my slice!"

I quickly stated my philosophy and asked the man to approach the ball much like he would if he were in the "batters box." We discussed fundamentals, then I asked him what went through his mind when he laced a single down the first baseline – he immediately replied, "Hell, I just aimed and hit it there!"

With that swing thought in mind, former Red Sox slugger Ted Williams gave a hearty laugh and laced a few 5-irons directly into right field without a slice during a lesson that lasted only 15 minutes, but will be remembered by this PGA Professional for a lifetime.

Bill May
Head Professional
Riverside Municipal Golf Course
Portland, Maine

Misplaced PING

Following a long day of business and networking on the floor of the PGA Merchandise Show in Orlando, Fla., in the early '90s, my wife and I joined my partner and fellow PGA member Clark Luis for a bite to eat at the '50s diner on the main floor of the Peabody Hotel. Since the hotel was very busy with the exposition crowd at this time, we were forced to wait in line.

My wife recognized the gray-haired man standing in front of us as the world-renowned PING golf manufacturer Karsten Solheim. After exchanging some pleasantries we began to discuss a particular left-handed PING 3-wood, which Clark owned, with the serial number 000001. Mr. Solheim gave us a look of total disbelief and explained that this could not be possible since it was the practice of the company to retain the first five editions of each model for the companies private PING collection. We assured him the club did exist and in fact, was in Clark's bag sitting outside in the trunk of the rental car. Clark had placed an order for a left-handed 3-wood with a PING representative before the club had even been made, which may account for his receiving a first edition. Clark had not noticed the serial number on the club for quite some time. Mr. Solheim went to his table bemused at our audacity in claiming possession of such a club. However, following dinner, I guess his curiosity got the best of him and he returned to our table and asked if we would show him the club. Without hesitation we left the girls to their coffee and headed to the parking lot.

As a PGA Professional, PING and in particular, its founder Karsten Solheim, will always hold a special place in my mind as a company that created a wonderful product to enhance the sport of golf. However, my lasting recollection of the man will be that of a curious collector, with his head stuck in the trunk of a car in the parking lot of the Peabody Hotel, offering my partner the world in exchange for a first edition PING golf club … and wondering how it was ever shipped, by mistake, from his plant. Clark refused to sell him the club, for any price, as it was his favorite 3-wood.

By the way … Clark still owns the club.

George R. Petrole
PGA Professional
Lehighton, Pa.

Always Listen to Dad's Advice

Growing up in the Atlanta area, my family had no exposure to golf at all. In fact, I was the first person in the family to play the game. I improved enough to finally play professional golf and I was fortunate to play at the Atlanta Classic in my first year on the PGA Tour.

The course was only 25 minutes from my home, so I decided to invite my dad, who had never seen me play, to come and watch me. Dad followed me around for two days, but I didn't play very well and I missed the cut. On the way home with my mom, Dad leaned forward from the back seat, patted my shoulder, and said, "Son, I don't know anything about golf, but if I were you, I would try to hit it a little closer to the flags on the green."

Larry Nelson
Winner of Three Major Championships
Marietta, Ga.

Patty Berg (left), joined by Hall of Famers Babe Didrikson Zaharias and Louise Suggs in a playful tug of the team trophy they won at the 1953 World Championship of Golf in Akron, Ohio.

Les Bolstad

Throughout my career I have had the good fortune to have been helped by any number of PGA Professionals, not the least of whom was the late Les Bolstad.

Having won the USGA's Public Links Amateur Championship in 1926, Les Bolstad was a superb player. He qualified for and played in the U.S. Open in 1930 and 1931, and also was the winner of multiple Minnesota Open Championships. He was an excellent teacher of the game as well, and in addition to his duties at both public and private golf courses over the years, he served as the longtime coach of the University of Minnesota men's golf team and was so revered that today the university's golf course is named for him.

For me, he was my swing doctor. At any point in my playing career if I felt something going sour, or became aware of a glitch in my swing I felt I was unable to remedy, I ran to Les Bolstad as fast as my feet could carry me. Not once did he fail me.

He was one of my earliest teachers, probably the one with whom I spent the most time and worked the hardest. He was patient and understanding, yet demanded dedication, concentration, and the willingness to devote many hours to practice and yet more practice. He always called me Patricia, rarely Patty, and from him I learned one of the game's harsh truths.

If I hit a bad shot, even one that really wasn't bad but nonetheless was less than satisfactory, he would say, "You hit that shot, Patricia. No one else hit it. You hit it. Just you, Patricia, all by yourself." I still can hear in my mind, his voice driving home the point that golf is an introspective solo, and that when on the course you can be surrounded by thousands of people yet still be alone.

On the other hand, when I hit a good shot, especially a beauty, he would have me repeat aloud as the ball flew off in the distance, "Patricia Berg hit that shot. Patricia Berg hit it. Nobody but Patricia Berg." Years afterward, in fact throughout my career, whenever I hit a good shot I would find myself smiling inwardly and thinking "Patty Berg hit that shot, nobody but Patty Berg."

To this day whenever I think of Les Bolstad, I thank him with all my heart.

Patty J. Berg
Winner of 15 LPGA Major Championships
Fort Myers, Fla.

It's All You Got in the Bag

Being a member of The PGA of America for 18 years has afforded me many fantastic golfing opportunities. As a golf professional who has Irish roots, playing on the hallowed golfing ground of the Royal Portrush Golf Club in Portrush, Northern Ireland, was a chance of a lifetime for me, my brother, John, and my father, James. One such memorable round of golf happened while playing the beautiful Dunluce Links course at Royal Portrush for the first time.

It was a cool, windy March afternoon. By the time we reached the back nine, the weather had turned ever colder, the wind more brisk, and rain had begun to fall. Of course, we were well prepared – we donned our rain suits and played on. We turned and headed toward the sea, playing "Skerries," beginning on the par-4, 371-yard 13th. Normally a drive and a short iron, this day, into a strong headwind, it required a good drive and a mid-iron approach. By now, the sky had darkened, the wind had increased, and the temperature had dropped noticeably.

Of course, the locals knew what that meant; a short-lived, but fierce, squall was blowing in off the North Atlantic. As John and I putted out on 13 and headed to the 14th tee, the 4 ball ahead of us (members) had already taken shelter from the squall in a hut built into the dune behind the 14th teeing ground.

Now, the 14th at Royal Portrush, aptly named "Calamity," is a very precise hole, even on a calm day! This par-3 measures 213 yards, with a carry over an intimidating gully of 190 yards. Anything to the right of the green drops literally straight down, a good 50 feet or more. Bogey is a great score from there and certainly far higher scores are common. The green sits like a plateau. Miss it right – you know what. Miss it left – there is a "bailout" area, where a par can be had with a deft pitch and putt. Beware, Calamity can be just that.

96

The members in the hut yelled out at us to, "Go ahead and play through!" Apparently, they knew something that we didn't. Searching in the back pocket of my rain pants for the scorecard, I pulled it out to get a yardage. Just at that moment, a voice with a thick Irish brogue pierced through the driving wind and rain. "Doonut bother lookin' at the card, laddie … it's awl ya gut in the bog."

John and I turned and looked at each other knowing right away that what we just heard was so true and so timely. We could only chuckle nervously knowing that the task at hand required special attention. With no hesitation, we both plucked our drivers from the bag.

It was my honor and as the ball left the clubface, I knew it had been struck pure and true. Off the ball flew, never leaving the flagstick, battling the elements, coming safely to rest on the green some 30 feet beyond the pin. Now it was John's turn and he did not disappoint. His tee shot was also beautifully struck and rocketed off through the squall, finding the green, nearer the pin than mine! We were thrilled to have hit two such wonderful shots under those trying conditions, but even sweeter was the fact that they were witnessed by the "dwellers" of the hut. They shouted, "Well done!" and off we trudged.

Later, in the clubhouse after the round, now sitting with our father, James, we were chatting with the members who had played that day about how the course played, the weather, local color and such. My brother and I were surprised to hear how others who had played that day had seen our shots, on this hole or that hole, and remarked how well we had played the famous course. There we were, father and sons, so near to the birthplace of our great grandfather. It truly was a memory to last a lifetime.

James W. Von Lossow
PGA Professional
Seattle, Wash.

Joe's Kindness

At the age of 12, I became totally enamored with the game of golf. I took a job picking up balls from the range and running errands after school at a par-60, public golf course named Lake Chabot, located in Vallejo, Calif. My dream was to become a PGA Tour Player someday and my job allowed me to practice almost every day. Our professional at Lake Chabot was Joe Mortara, Jr. and he was both my teacher and my employer. His father, Joe Mortara, Sr., was the PGA Professional at a neighboring public course named Blue Rock Springs. Joe Sr. had a reputation amongst the kids, myself included, of being a crotchety old man who did not like children.

One day, I was practicing chip shots at the Blue Rock Springs practice green, when Joe Sr. approached me. He had often seen me practicing on the course but had never approached me before. Immediately, a knot formed in my stomach as I was sure that he was going to reprimand me for something and tell me to get lost. Imagine my surprise when he started talking to me, asking me about myself and my game – perhaps my total dedication to practice impressed him. In a short time, he was teaching me a variety of shots and explaining to me when they should be used on the course.

After about 30 minutes of free instruction, Joe asked me if I liked any other sports besides golf and I told him that I also enjoyed football. He then asked me if I would like to go see the 49ers play in San Francisco. I was stunned! But, of course, I said, "Yes," and we made the arrangements.

The following Sunday afternoon, at Candlestick Park, will be forever etched in my memory. We sat at the 50-yard line and Joe treated me to every snack I could eat. For as long as I live, I will never forget the kindness that Joe Mortara, Sr. bestowed upon me that week.

Joe Sr. passed away many years ago, but his memory lives on every time I follow his example and walk out to the putting green, on a sunny afternoon, to introduce myself to a young junior golfer and give him or her a few free tips. Thank you, Joe.

Larry D. Thornhill
PGA Professional
Colchester, Conn.

The Impossible Putt

As a PGA Professional, one of my most rewarding experiences was to work with the Special Olympics. I had the honor of participating in the 1999 games in Tennessee. One morning, athletes and coaches from many states convened at the Golf House in Tennessee. The green there was large and undulated and presented a great opportunity to find a medium length putt that seemed totally impossible to make. When even our PGA instructors were having trouble even getting close, I made the general announcement to all Special Olympians that, indeed, it was the "impossible putt" and was worth a $1 million check to anyone who could hole it in "one."

Everyone took the opportunity to attempt the "impossible putt" and it became the center of attention. On the second day of camp, I was deep in conversation with a couple of my fellow PGA Professionals, when the loudest, shrillest scream imagined came from the area of the green. Danny Dasis, a Special Olympic athlete from Mississippi, had made the "impossible putt" and was going ballistic. Ten athletes around him were screaming as loudly as Danny. I turned around just in time to brace myself for Danny's leap into my arms. There is no proper way to prepare yourself to catch a 200-pound man running full speed and leaping on top of you. What I ended up with was his legs wrapped around my waist, his arms around my chest and arms, pinning them to my side, and Danny kissing me repeatedly. Of course, I couldn't see anyone's reaction, but I understand that several people fell to the ground from laughing so hard.

I can honestly say that prior to that "impossible putt" I had never been kissed on the lips by a grown man. Soon our story was circulating around the Olympic villages and a photo of Danny kissing me appeared in the local paper. I guess I did get the last laugh though, since my million dollar check bounced.

Jesse Weeks
PGA Member
Head Professional
Orgill Park Country Club
Millington, Tenn.

Mr. Wrench

A few years ago, I was working in the golf shop at Oswego Lake Country Club and a brand new attendant started his first "solo" round in the bag room. One of our members, an honorable judge, appeared at the door of the bag room and said, "spike wrench." Our new attendant nodded his head, and then ran down one row of bags and up the other. Noticeably frustrated he repeated the routine a second time.

Meanwhile, the honorable judge was standing patiently wondering why it was such an ordeal to simply find a wrench to tighten up a loose spike.

Finally, the attendant came back to the judge and said, "I'm sorry Mr. Wrench, I can't find your clubs!"

Coralee Jorgensen
Head Professional
Westward Ho Country Club
Sioux Falls, S.D.

I Heard It Coming!

I am the teaching professional at Old South Country Club in Lothian, Md., which is directly under the flight pattern for Andrews Air Force Base. As a result, we have lots of aircraft flying over our course.

One day I was contacted by Tom Clancy, the famous author of *The Hunt for Red October*, *Patriot Games,* and other military based novels. Tom wanted to take a playing lesson with me on the course. Due to all the research he has done for his books, Tom is an expert in military equipment and as we moved about the course, I was amazed with Tom's uncanny ability to identify aircraft overhead simply by sound.

Our lesson went well and Tom booked another playing lesson three weeks later. In checking my lesson book, I realized that one of our regular members had scheduled a tee time immediately following Tom's lesson. I made a note to inform the member of my lesson so he could play through if we were slow.

On the day of the lesson the member arrived early and due to a superstitious quirk, wanted to purchase one dozen Titleist DT's with red No. 3s only. Our staff had to open other boxes and pull the No. 3 balls to make up a dozen for our member, but we did it.

Mr. Clancy arrived right on time and we went out for our lesson. We moved along at a good pace and the member behind us with the Titleist DT No. 3 red balls did not need to play through.

As Tom prepared to hit a fairway shot at the seventh hole, we could hear the "thwack" of a golf ball being struck on the sixth tee.

Suddenly, we heard the cry, "Fore!" and I told Tom to watch out for those Titleist DT No. 3 red balls ... "they can be deadly."

A second later I heard Tom yell and a golf ball landed right next to his leg. Tom looked down at the ball and exclaimed, "Hey, it's a Titleist DT with a red No. 3! How'd you know that?"

I explained, "I heard it coming."

Because I did not give Tom enough information I think, to this day, he believes I really have the ability to differentiate golf balls in flight by their sound.

Jon Magarace
PGA Teaching Professional
Old South Country Club
Lothian, Md.

Keep Looking

All of my life, I have been fascinated by the game of golf and have closely followed the accomplishments of many of the masters. What I have learned from watching the professionals is that they have a unique ability to "bounce back" from a bad shot or ugly lie. All of the golf professionals I have worked with have made the interesting point – never give up hope. If you hit a bad shot, take a deep breath and move on. Your next shot can be a great one.

As a teenager growing up in Logansport, Ind., I was learning to play golf and would take instruction from anyone who would teach me. This included taking lessons from one of my schoolmates, Don, who was a few years older than I was and played on the high school golf team. Don was somewhat of a local idol for me, and his insight and teaching ability helped shape my future in golf.

One day, Don and I were playing Dykeman Golf Course, the public course in Logansport, and we came to the ninth tee, a 540-yard hole, par-5, with a slight dogleg right and a generous driving area. There were woods and out of bounds to the right. Don had the honors so he teed off first. He hit his drive to the right so we expected it could be out of bounds. But, ever the hopeful youth, he elected not to hit a provisional. We went down the fairway to the right side of the driving area and looked, but the ball was not to be found. Don returned to the tee to hit his provisional. This time he hit it "straight as a die" and right on the screws. In those days, woods actually had screws to hold the inserts in the face of wooden heads (and still sound better than the "clink" the current clubs make). It was a nice drive, about 280 yards.

Don went down to find his ball and it was dead in the middle of the fairway. Don remarked that he would need to do something spectacular to break 40 for this side. Then he withdrew his 3-wood from his bag and ripped his shot perilously close to the right side of the green with the woods and out of bounds … a courageous shot. We walked toward the green to find our balls, and found mine but not Don's. We proceeded to search the fairway in front of the green and in the traps to the right and left. We searched behind the green and in an adjacent tee-box area. Nothing. On a whim, I decided to look in the hole. I walked over and peered in, sure enough – there was a ball. I asked Don what he was playing, he told me, and I reached in and pulled out his ball. Net score for Don, a dandy little birdie for a tidy 36. Even par for that side. So, where is the lesson? As so many of my golf professionals have always told me, "Never give up hope."

Mark E. Dinius
Valencia, Calif.

Why You Should Use a Golf Professional

Recently, I was watching *Academy Live* on The Golf Channel in my family room as my wife prepared dinner a few feet away in the kitchen. As I sipped a bit of Merlot, I listened to Butch Harmon discuss how he helped make Tiger Woods the greatest player in the world. Butch was providing some very valuable swing tips and I decided to follow along. I keep a 3-iron in with our fireplace tools for exactly this reason.

With my PING iron in hand, I adjusted my grip as Butch advised. I opened my left foot about 1/2 inch so my club could clear a bit easier on the follow-through and moved my imaginary ball position just a bit more forward in my stance.

I felt my address position was now perfect. As I watched and listened intently to Butch and Peter Kessler, the host, I drew my club back very slowly with a focus on maintaining my triangle. My downswing was absolutely perfect. At impact, my club face was totally square and I knew my imaginary ball would have gone about 180 yards. I really felt it was a great shot and I envisioned it stopping no more than a few feet from the pin.

I distinctly remember maintaining my text book triangle as I entered my follow-through … right up to the time that I drove my 3-iron into the television picture tube.

The explosion was enormous. My wife stopped screaming about 20 minutes after the fire department left. While I missed dinner that evening, I did learn a very valuable lesson. If you want to improve your golf swing, television is wonderful, but it's best to seek the assistance of a golf professional.

Tom Murphy
Dallas, Texas

Curtis Strange, the 23rd United States Ryder Cup Captain, guided the American Team at The Belfry in 2001.

My Mentor

Chandler Harper was one of my greatest supporters and did so much to improve my golf fundamentals.

When my father passed away when I was 14 and I needed someone to watch over me, Chandler became my mentor and golf instructor. He was a PGA Champion and the logical choice for me to turn to. Chandler believed that training was like a pyramid that you build upon – you had to have the foundation or you could never get to the top. He was very good and kept to the basics, and we did not get too technical over the years. He knew what I was doing right and what I was doing wrong.

While people would criticize my intensity, Chandler liked it, because he was that way, too.

Chandler always wanted me to have a very strong left grip because both he, and his good friend, Sam Snead, did. The only time I played with a strong left grip was when I played with him – I wanted to make him proud of me. When Chandler was not around, I would switch back to my weak left hand, which was comical because I never played worth a damn when I did that.

Chandler was a magician with parts of the game and had an incredible touch with his hands. He would chip, not blast, out of bunkers. He was one of the best chippers you have ever seen – he was in a category with Steve Ballesteros or Tom Watson.

In 1976 I was going to the finals of the North and South Amateur and I called Chandler the night before because I was as nervous as could be. He got right to the point and said, "What you have done until now does not mean a damn. You have got to win tomorrow to make it worth something. I don't care how well you play match play, it's not worth anything until you win the finals." I went on to win, and he was right.

Chandler showed me that you always need someone to look up to. Bobby Cruickshank was someone Chandler respected, and Chandler and Sam Snead have been good friends over the years. Sam was my hero when I was growing up. I studied and admired his swing and now I tell my boys, "If Sam Snead didn't do it in his swing, then it's not good enough for you."

Curtis Strange
Winner of Two Major Championships
2001 U.S. Ryder Cup Captain
Williamsburg, Va.

A Low Key Guest

It felt like I was standing on the 16th tee at Cypress Point for the first time. My knees were knocking and I was tense all over. I don't think I'd be more nervous if I were teeing off at the Open. I was facing my first shot while playing with President Bill Clinton at the Orinda Country Club in California.

On the Wednesday prior to the Saturday presidential visit, an advance team from the Secret Service arrived at the course for a preliminary inspection. On Thursday, a group of agents arrived and installed three special phone lines and turned one of the club's third floor apartments into Communications Central. On Friday afternoon, the lead agent delivered a list of items needed for the president – among them were 17 golf cars marked with tags such as "Explosive Ordinance Disposal," "Counter Assault Team Forward," "Counter Sniper 1," and "Presidential Protection Division 1." On Saturday, Secret Service teams buzzed all around the club installing antennae and phone lines on each of the golf cars.

Shortly thereafter, we saw the presidential caravan coming up the hill. It consisted of several Highway Patrol cruisers, two limousines, several black Suburbans, an ominous looking black van with its windows blacked out, several more police cruisers, and 10 motorcycle police.

The President's administrators asked our staff to keep his visit "low key." Thank God, what I just described is "low key." I do not think our club could have stood "high key!" As an 18-year PGA veteran, I did not let the pressure of having Secret Service agents with guns hidden in the trees rattle me. I had an impressive birdie-birdie finish to shoot even par-72. As for the President, he carded a respectable 84.

The day was filled with moments of hectic excitement and ended with one last emotional charge as President Clinton exited the 18th green, waving goodbye, and moved on to his next "low key" destination.

Paul LaGoy
PGA Professional
Orinda (Calif.) Country Club

Joe's Return

As the manager of Learning Center Programs at The PGA facility in Port St. Lucie, Fla., I have worked with many golfing students, but Joe Johnson's accomplishment stands out in my memory as one of the greatest.

One day he said, "I'm so excited about standing on the tee again and hitting the ball, even if it's only 60 yards." Joe used to hit the ball 200 yards and played three times a week until he had a stroke and lost the use of most of his left side. When we met he was nervous and scared about swinging a club with the use of only one arm and what people might think about him.

Listening to Joe, I understood his concerns – but with my experience having worked with golfers who have encountered injuries, I knew he could do it if he put his mind to it. We worked together as a team and after a few weeks of instruction, Joe was on his way to playing golf again. We made some swing modifications as well as equipment changes. We strengthened his balance and worked on weight training with his physical therapist. In time, Joe's confidence as well as his ability greatly improved.

Today, Joe can drive 80 yards and this accomplishment is truly amazing. Joe is one of the many students with whom I have shared in the rehabilitation process to regain their golf status. But, what is really interesting is that I am the one who keeps learning that anyone can do anything, if they put their mind to it. He taught me that sometimes the hardest door to open is your own front door and with a little hard work a lot can be accomplished with your life. Thanks, Joe.

Judy Alvarez
Manager of Learning Center Programs
Port St. Lucie, Fla.

Waiting for Loof

Professional golfers are a wonderful breed. Not only do they work hard, but they play hard. They also have more integrity than most because the game itself demands it. Perhaps this is why many are a bit gullible.

Not long after my arrival from England, I accepted a position as the Teaching Director at the Grenelefe Golf Resort in Central Florida. April Fool's Day was upon us and I had the opportunity to play a little prank on one of my teaching professionals. This gentleman shall remain nameless, so as to protect him from the ribbing he may take from his fellow professionals.

He was a very clean cut and enthusiastic individual who would go to any lengths to secure a lesson. Exactly the sort of person you'd like to play a prank on. I informed this colleague that a guest from the hotel had called and said that he was looking for a lesson. He was attending a seminar at the resort and due to his hectic schedule, the only time available to him would be a 6:30 a.m. session. Would it be possible to arrange something for him? He was quite prepared, due to the early hour, to pay a premium for the lesson.

With the image of a lesson and a huge tip, my colleague jumped at the opportunity. I told my assistant that the gentleman's name was "Loof Lirpa" and that he was a visitor from Denmark who spoke English very poorly. I arranged for the professional and Mr. Lirpa to meet on the practice tee at 6:30 a.m. and suggested that it would not be hard to spot one another at that early hour.

So, on April 1st, a particularly cool, frosty, Florida spring morning, my instructor got up at 5:00 a.m. and arrived at the range about six to meet Mr. Lirpa. At 7:30, I received a phone call from my rather frustrated teaching professional telling me that the client had not shown up. Furthermore, upon checking with registration at the hotel, there was no guest registered under the name "Loof Lirpa." Acting rather surprised, I offered him my commiseration and said, "You just can't trust these damn foreigners."

On seeing him later that morning, needless to say, he was still in a rather grumpy mood and after listening to his grumbling for a while, I started chuckling. I asked him to take the name "Loof Lirpa" and spell it backwards. After a couple of seconds, the penny dropped. He looked at me for a few seconds more, then said, "You're right, you just can't trust these damn foreigners!"

David Leadbetter
PGA Teaching Professional
David Leadbetter Golf Academy
Orlando, Fla.

Many Thanks to Marty

In 1955, I was working as a school teacher in Cincinnati, when I met my husband Paul, who was employed by the Dover Corporation, as a design engineer. Paul was an avid golfer and in 1968, I decided to take up golf so that Paul and I could spend more time together. I took my first group golf lesson with Marty Kavanaugh, who was the teaching professional at the Miami Whitewater Golf Course.

I did well in the group program so I continued on with Marty, taking private lessons. Marty focused on the basics. I'll always remember him telling me that the "key to a strong swing is in setting up to the ball correctly." When my game struggled, Marty was always there with just the right tip to fix my problem. My game improved with Marty's help, so Paul and I started playing together on a regular basis. Paul and I even began playing in club tournaments and Marty's advice before my tournaments was invaluable. Marty spent a lot of time teaching me the Rules of Golf and golf etiquette. I think his integrity and his exceptional professionalism have rubbed off on me because I truly believe I am a better person having known Marty all these years.

In 1996, after teaching school for 35 years, I decided to retire. Paul and I were looking forward to playing golf together every day but five months after my retirement, Paul passed away. Obviously, I was devastated. I don't think I ever felt so alone, but I had my golf to help me. I began working at Walden Pond Country Club in Cincinnati, two days a week, as a starter. Because of Marty's teaching, our members were impressed with my knowledge of course rules, golf etiquette, golf car rules, and basic golf information. I have now been working at Walden Pond for four years. I play golf five days a week and spend six months a year playing in Bonita Springs, Fla.

My handicap is now 11 and I've had many wonderful accomplishments in the past few years including playing in several tournaments. Golf has brought so much happiness to my life. Paul and I shared golf with our three sons as they grew up and now I've started my granddaughter on golf lessons. I miss Paul very much, but my golf has made it possible for me to have a wonderful life. I know that none of this would have been possible without the dedication and help of Marty Kavanaugh, a great professional.

Georgia Wilder
Bonita Springs, Fla.

Rules Are Rules

After she retired from the LPGA Tour, Donna Horton White sponsored an annual LPGA Pro-Am at the Wellington (Fla.) Country Club to benefit The Special Olympics.

Donna is an exceptional human being and was a favorite among her fellow professionals. For this reason, many celebrity players always showed up at her event to provide an excellent field. It was a treat for us "amateurs" to play golf with these marvelous young women; something you looked forward to, something to look back upon with fond golfing memories.

Over the years, I played with Laurie Rinker, Sandra Haynie, JoAnne "Big Mama" Carner, Beth Zimmerman, Janet Coles, Dale Eggeling and many others.

One year I will never forget involved Sandra Palmer, an LPGA "Hall-of-Famer." While she was not as long a hitter as some of the other tour players (after all, she was only 90 pounds soaking wet), she did hit the ball with amazing accuracy and could putt the lights out. We were having a really good day. The scramble format had yielded us a nice, eleven-under score going to the 16th tee. Marshals told us they had not heard lower scores from the groups that preceded us. "Let's win this thing," said Sandra enthusiastically.

The 16th was a par-3 with a huge hourglass-shaped green surrounded by sand traps and fronted by a lake. It seemed that the pressure of a possible win was getting to us because the only ball safely on the 16th green was Sandra's. Unfortunately, she had pull-hooked it onto one end of the hourglass and the pin was located on the other.

My friend, Peter, was the designated "first" putter. He faced a 75-footer with a 15- or 20-foot swing from left to right. We all looked it over and voted on the line. "Let me take a look from the other side," I said and I walked to the other end of the green, getting down directly behind the hole. "Peter," I yelled, "you gotta hit way up on that hill. Try to roll it right over that old ball mark. Watch the pace. It will be very quick at the hole."

"OK," he replied as he set up over the ball. I was standing by the hole, watching carefully because I was next to putt and I wanted to go to school on his effort. His putt looked really good ... up the hill ... turned ... started down the fall line ... broke towards the hole ... pretty good speed. As I stood there, mesmerized, the unbelievable happened ... the ball went right into the hole!

Everybody was doing high-fives except Sandra Palmer. She slowly walked over to me, placed her hand on my shoulder and asked, "Warren, why didn't you pull the flag? You know there's a penalty if a putt goes in with the flag still in the hole!"

My jaw dropped open. I was devastated. "Sandra," I said, "it never occurred to me."

Of course, our half-hearted attempts to talk her out of charging our team the requisite two shot penalty for the rule fell on deaf (professional) ears.

You know the end of the story. We lost the tournament by one shot. The forgiving words of my teammates and the many hugs I got from Sandra throughout the rest of the day could not console me.

But, as bad as it was, I was very proud to be a part of the decision to "do the right thing." Sandra Palmer reinforced in all of us that day that the golf game is built on honesty and integrity and I thank her for that.

Warren Essner
Garden City Country Club
Garden City, Long Island

Club Professional Turned Bartender

Back in the mid '80s, I leased a clubhouse at Charmingfare Links in Candia, N.H. One year, late in the fall, I was approached by the local chief of police and was asked if I would serve dinner for about 50 chiefs of police for the County of Rockingham, N.H. The event was to be their annual election of officers for the upcoming year. With all the arrangements made, I lined up the help that would be needed to serve the dinner and tend the bar.

The day prior to the event, I was just finishing a round of golf with some members when I noticed some police cruisers parking in the lot and my wife waving her arms frantically for me to come immediately into the clubhouse. After putting out the 18th hole, I went in to find my wife yelling, "The police chiefs' dinner is tonight, not tomorrow!" Somehow, we had recorded the wrong date. Rich Thibeault, our club professional, was shutting down for the day and he asked me, "What are you going to do?" I realized that panic was the wrong reaction so I turned to Rich and said, "Rich, you are going to learn how to make mashed potatoes and stuffing to go along with a turkey." I then recruited the members who had played the round of golf with me to set the tables. Fortunately, we had a turkey in the cooler which we quickly got into the oven and my wife and another member cut the apple pie and sliced the cranberry sauce. After fixing the potatoes and stuffing, Rich moved out into the hall and became the bartender for the evening. Instead of having dinner first, I suggested getting the election of officers over so they could enjoy their dinner (so I could buy time for the turkey to cook!).

Rich, having started his day at 6 a.m., was truly a professional for staying with me and the club members for that evening. Because of him, it was a great success.

Rich is now the head professional at Concord Country Club in Concord, N.H. He ranks number one in their books and he ranks number one in mine. If he ever gets tired of being a golf professional I'll always have a spot for him as a banquet manager!

Joe Culleton
Big Cypress Golf and Country Club
Lakeland, Fla.

Byron Nelson, in 1945, during a historic 18-victory season.

Tribute to Byron

Byron Nelson is, undisputedly, one of the greatest legends in the history of golf. Even as he approaches 90 years of age, he is still active and playing. Every now and then, Byron will come down to the golf school named for him for a photo shoot, or to do a book signing, and this is always a highlight with the students.

One day, Byron felt like hitting a few balls. The Masters was approaching and he would, once again, be opening the event as a ceremonial starter. All the champions wanted to get some practice shots in before the Masters, and so did Byron. To help him, I teed up ball after ball as Byron took some swings with his 3-wood. About 20 students watched in awe as the then-88-year-old shaped shot after shot with a little draw, splitting the middle of the practice range. Through all of this, Byron carried on a dialogue with the students watching the legend.

One interested student asked him how he had corrected his slice. Many of the students, who had experienced their own problems with slicing, eagerly waited for some insight from the sage Hall of Famer. Byron paused, paused some more, lifted his finger as if to answer, stopped, and paused again. You could almost sense him going back through 80 years of playing the game. Finally, he turned to the student and answered, "I never sliced." With that, the golf school went wild.

Shawn Humphries
Owner & Teaching Professional
SH Golf Inc.
Dallas, Texas

Score One for a Ridey

During my 10 years as a teaching professional at the Medinah Country Club in Illinois, we would initiate each new season with a special program for women new to the sport of golf. I will always remember one season in particular since that program broke new ground in golf and caused us to actually create a new scoring system. I might add that I am led to believe that other professionals in other clubs around the world have experienced this same unique scoring system. The season to be remembered involved 12 women who had never played golf before and registered in our program. This represented a much larger group than the average four to six who typically land in this category.

The curriculum was geared to be as simple as possible. In addition to elementary basics and game improvement techniques it featured etiquette, rules, registration procedures, location of the practice facility, and other very basic golf procedures. Even though the club had an active caddie program, using a golf car was the popular practice with this particular group. So, an additional part of the instructional program was on the operation and safety rules of golf cars.

The beginner's group met twice a week. After just the third week, the ladies wanted to not only play but were demanding some competition. Each time they played they held their own type of scoring procedure depending on that day's competition. Seldom did they play a complete nine holes and more often these "rounds" lasted just three or six holes. Nevertheless, our staff wanted to encourage their participation and frequently inquired if everything was going well and if they were enjoying their round.

This discussion was usually with the group's "official event scorekeeper" who reported, "So-and-so had three Rideys, or so-and-so had four Rideys." After reviewing a few of these scoring reports, I simply had to beg the question, "Please explain to me, what is a 'Ridey'?"

The scorekeeper's explanation was simple: anytime someone hit the ball far enough for you to ride to the next shot, a "Ridey" was recorded. You can guess the rest ... the season-ending prizes and awards went to the golfer with the most "Rideys" on her scorecard.

Bob Hickman
PGA Professional
Jupiter, Fla.

Truck Chip

About six years ago I was playing golf with a group of friends and on the advice of my golf professional we were playing different courses to improve our games. This day we were on the 16th hole of a small public course located in a state park in Charleston, W.Va. A main road, with significant traffic, runs directly through the park and is parallel with the 160-yard, par-3, 16th hole. On this particular day, traffic was at a standstill. As we were walking up to the tee, we were commenting on the "legality" of a large truck that was stuck in the traffic, right next to the green. It was an older truck but it had some of the biggest tires we had ever seen on a vehicle. This truck could have gotten out of the traffic jam simply by driving over the other cars.

My friend, Shannon, was the first one to tee off and he hit a wicked slice that was targeting directly at the truck. We all gasped in horror at the thought of our golf ball crashing into this vehicle and some large man getting out of his "pride and joy" monster truck with a shotgun and a bad attitude. As miracles would have it, Shannon's ball hit the passenger side front tire, thankfully, instead of any metal or glass. With a loud "thump" the ball then shot back, bounced once on the fairway, rolled up on the green like a perfect chip shot, and right into the hole. The guy in the truck never looked over and he had no idea what had happened. I still laugh to this day every time I see the wooden plaque that Shannon bought to display his hole-in-one Titleist, complete with the black "scuff" mark from the truck tire. After that day though, I did tell my professional that I felt more comfortable playing my own course.

Allen Bibbee
Hurricane, W.Va.

Warren's World

The game of golf has been good to Warren Orlick, an 87-year-old Birmingham, Mich., resident and retired golf professional. Now he is returning the favor. During his nearly 80 years in golf, Warren has met most of the games greats, including Bobby Jones, Ben Hogan and Jack Nicklaus. Arnold Palmer once flew Warren home on his private jet because he was going to be late for work. He has attended every Masters golf tournament since 1954, played with the 1953 Ryder Cup Team, and was president of The PGA of America.

More recently, Warren has decided to use his knowledge of the game to make a profound difference in the lives of disabled golfers. He teaches patients at St. Joseph's Hospital, in Pontiac, to cope with a disability and return to the game after suffering a debilitating injury such as paralysis or amputation. Warren first realized he had a knack for working with disabled golfers during World War II, where many of the patients were amputees. He demonstrated his ability to hit balls with one arm or standing on one leg, convincing them that they, too, could return to golf.

Warren begins his classes by relating how he suffered nerve damage in his left hand while undergoing quadruple bypass heart surgery. Unable to grip a club, he invented a Velcro golf glove that allowed him to once again hold a club and play the game. His return to golf has inspired him to help others. He teaches disabled golfers to play with the aid of a special car that has a swivel seat and a special suspension system that allows them complete access to the course, including the ability to negotiate bunkers and drive on the greens. One of his students claims he is a great teacher "because he is patient and he understands what we are going through."

Synergy is the joining of separate, distinct entities that come together

126

and create something altogether different. This is what happened when Warren combined his talents as a golf professional and a therapy patient and the Adaptive Golf Program was born. White Lake Oaks Country Club honors Warren annually by holding the Warren Orlick Inclusive Golf Open for disabled golfers.

Marian Stone
Westport, Conn.

What Do I Do?

Back in the late 1960s, I was the head professional and director of instruction at Oakway Golf Course, a very busy daily fee operation in Eugene, Ore. In those years we had the largest golf school west of the Mississippi River and it was not unusual for me to teach 200 or 300 people a week in group lessons.

One Thursday afternoon around 3 p.m., I was finished teaching a bit early and rather than go home for dinner, I called my wife to tell her that I was going out to play nine holes. I hung up the phone, picked up my carry bag, slipped on my spikes (not even bothering to tie them), and headed for the first tee where a middle-aged couple was just preparing to tee off. I didn't recognize them, as we had a great deal of transient play, but I asked if they would mind if I played along for nine holes. They consented and I told them to go ahead and hit, as I needed to tie my shoes and loosen up.

The first hole played from an elevated tee. It was a 515-yard, slight dogleg left, par-5. A creek ran down the right side and trees bordered the left. I could usually reach the green in two with a pair of good shots. While I tied my shoes, the man hit a very nice drive about 230 yards from the white tees. That was encouraging. His wife played from the red markers, which in those less sensitive days, were placed only five yards ahead of the white tees. She hit a good drive, as well. Well, I thought to myself, this is going to be an enjoyable round. I stationed myself at the blue markers, made a few practice swings, and addressed the ball, preparing to demonstrate how a professional (although they did not know I was) hits a powerful drive. It was a powerful swing, but not a powerful drive. The swing had velocity, but unfortunately, was about 1½ inches too high. I caught the very top of the ball, causing it to roll slowly forward across the tee-box, first between the white markers, then the red, until it rolled over the edge partly down the hill ending up halfway between the crest and base of the tee. I stared at the result in disbelief and since I did not take mulligans, I walked down to my ball and assumed my stance in the longish grass on the severe downhill slope. Trying to make up for such a bad drive, I made a mighty swing with my 2-iron and proceeded to shank it toward the creek.

Now really embarrassed, we all walked toward my ball. I tried to lighten the mood by asking my new friends where they were from. They replied, "Wausau, Wisconsin," and I complimented them on living in such a fine state with such friendly people. After reaching my just-played errant shot, I noticed they now took care to stand safely aside as I selected a 3-wood for my next amazing shot. Now, I had to really rip one in order to get close enough to hit the green in regulation. I did rip it. However, it was a wild hook that screamed across the fairway into the woods on the left. As we continued our walk together toward their tee shots, I asked the gentleman what he did for a living. He said, "I run a wholesale lumber yard." Then he asked, "What do you do for a living?" There was silence for the next few seconds. It was decision time. Did I or didn't I have the nerve to tell him the truth? I did not! I rationalized that if I told him that I was a professional golfer he would not believe me. Worse, if he did, he would never choose to take lessons at our course.

So, we enjoyed each other's company for the rest of the round as I played under the pretense of being a University of Oregon professor.

Dr. Gary Wiren
PGA Master Professional
Trump International Golf Club
West Palm Beach, Fla.

Swing Shift

I began on the PGA Tour in June of 1960. A few years later, I ran into a snag – I went from July of 1963 to July of 1964 not making one 36-hole cut.

My attorney and sponsor, Mike Sterbick, wouldn't let me quit. He suggested that I see Ockie Eliason at the Lakewood Driving Range in Tacoma. Ockie gave me a swing change and my game changed overnight. I won the B.C. Open in July 1964 and never looked back.

I went on to win three times on The PGA Tour and was a member of the 1969 Ryder Cup Team.

Ockie turned my game around.

The point of the story is that, sometimes, when all seems lost, it only takes the help of a true professional like Ockie to make a few adjustments in your game, or life, for things to improve. Do not be afraid to ask for help – you just might like the results.

Ken Still
PGA Senior Tour Professional
Fircrest, Wash.

My Dad in Bhutan

Golf professionals are well known for their unique encounters around the world with all sorts of interesting people – but my dad, Carl Marinello, a PGA Professional, is right up there at the top of the list. In the late 1960s when much of America was caught up in the pursuit of "inner peace," Dad was working in the New York City area running our family's combination practice range and golf recreational center.

In 1986, Dad read an item in a PGA of America employment bulletin about the People to People Sports Committee, Inc. established by President Eisenhower in 1956 to encourage international understanding and cooperation through athletics. They were looking for a PGA Professional skilled in teaching, to spend four months in Bhutan, a country just south of Tibet, helping prepare a Bhutanese golf team for the 1986 Asian Games in Seoul.

Dad decided to accept the position and in June of 1986, he arrived in the Himalayan country of Bhutan. Most of the nation existed much the same as it did 200 years ago. The people wore the same clothes, ate the same foods, and held the same jobs as their ancestors. Dad described the country as "not far removed from the 12th century," with most of the people being farmers. After meeting his perspective golf team and after visiting their mountain golf course, Dad came to the sad conclusion that it would be very difficult to build a golf team for the Asian Games from this remote part of the world. It would be almost impossible using their crude golf course. So, Dad took his team to neighboring India to play golf on grass greens. It was 110 degrees every day. There were vultures on the courses, goats in the sand traps, and people would wash their clothing in the water hazards. It was like something out of Kipling. Once the team learned that golf is a target-oriented game involving more finesse than raw power, they were fine. Dad used their tradition of meditation, which is so prevalent in that part of the world, to calm their game.

Forty-four nations participated in the games. The Bhutanese team started slowly, but came back strong to move into 11th place. Dressed in very colorful native Bhutanese dress they also established themselves as crowd favorites. On the last day of the tournament, they played their finest and jumped over China into 10th. Dad's fledgling team had pulled a stunning upset over China.

His Majesty, King Wangchuck, and the government were so impressed that they decided to reconstruct their golf course. Dad was there for both the dedication and when the Royal Bhutan Golf Course received its first golf car along with several sets of PING clubs. Dad would like to return to Bhutan as the club's golf director and national golf coach. He is learning as much as he can about Buddhist philosophy and the art of meditation and its potential as a teaching aid for golf in the United States. Dad talks about staying in Bhutan permanently. If he does, he will have gone full cycle: From a New York City golf professional with the hassles of the 20th century ... to someone content to live among people who exist much the same way they did centuries ago.

Tiffany Marinello
Cape Coral, Fla.

Lee Trevino, shown following a round in the late 1960s, won six major championships, including the 1974 and 1984 PGA Championships.

Sportsmanship Under Fire

As a member of the media following Lee Trevino at two different U.S. Opens, I observed two thoughtful displays of sportsmanship.

At the 1968 U.S. Open at Oak Hill Country Club, Trevino was battling Bert Yancey for the lead. On a green on the back nine, Yancey marked his ball, then re-marked it, to get his coin out of Trevino's putting line. When it was time for Yancey to putt, he put his ball down, forgetting to move the marker back to its proper original position. Trevino didn't forget. Though his words were out of earshot, it was evident that Trevino reminded Yancey to move the coin back to its original position. As it turned out, Trevino won that U.S. Open.

In the 1971 Open at Merion, an amateur, Jim Simons, was the leader during the third round as he addressed his tee shot on the 14th hole. Suddenly, but softly, as if he were a teaching professional giving a lesson, Trevino said, "Son, this game is tough enough without a two-shot penalty." Simons looked down and realized that his ball was teed up ahead of the markers. He re-teed his ball behind the markers. Trevino won that U.S. Open in a playoff with Jack Nicklaus.

Lee Trevino displayed true sportsmanship by helping his rivals when he didn't have to, and true skill by going on to win both U.S. Opens.

Dave Anderson
New York Times
1998 Recipient, PGA Lifetime Achievement Award in Journalism
Tenafly, N.J.

In "The Haig's" Image

In the late summer of 1999, I had the very good fortune to be cast as Walter Hagen in Robert Redford's film *The Legend of Bagger Vance*. I knew a bit about "The Haig" from various golf books and periodicals. I knew enough to slick back my hair, wear spiffy clothes with a tie, and deliver the lines of the audition scenes with unabashed, friendly confidence. I also recalled he had a wide stance. Not a lot of knowledge, but enough to help me win the role.

Upon arrival in Savannah, Ga., amid the frantic flurry of pre-production; hair and make-up meetings, wardrobe fittings, rehearsals, and lodging problems, I met "the guy who's teaching Matt Damon to play golf in five weeks." Enter PGA Master Professional Tim Moss who was to be instrumental in my research and work to portray Hagen. At Jekyll Island (which served as Krewe Island in the film) Tim handed me an old book written by "The Haig" himself.

It seems that, Leo Fraser, the godfather to Tim's son, had toured with the great Hagen. Leo drove the golf car, Hagen played the golf, and they split the proceeds. Leo got 50 bucks and Hagen got $500. At any rate, that book was a treasure trove in my efforts to flesh out the Hagen persona. It would have been useful if it was just the writings of "The Haig" himself, but at the start of each chapter was a quote from one of his contemporaries; sports writers, opponents, partners, and fellow competitors writing about Hagen from their point of view. Absolute gold!

Tim would also stand off camera when I was executing a golf shot for the film, and indicate with a thumbs-up or down whether I had successfully "Hagenized" it or not. What a comfort his keen eye was. In the first few weeks of filming, every time Tim saw me come out in the Hagen wardrobe, he would smile with delight and say, "You *are* Walter Hagen!" I am sure he doesn't realize what a powerful reinforcement to my process he was.

Tim was also near at hand on a freezing Kiawah Island morning when I had to peel off spikes and socks and enter a water hazard with an eight-foot alligator who had not eaten in over a month. He thought that was hilarious, but that's another tale.

When our filming was complete, I wanted to return Tim's rare book. He "borrowed it back" just long enough to write a beautiful dedication to me in it. He then handed it back to me saying, "You should have this." It is on my shelf now, a treasured gift, as is my enduring friendship with Mr. Moss.

Bruce McGill
"Walter Hagen"
The Legend of Bagger Vance
Los Angeles, Calif.

When the Going Gets Tough … the Tough Get Going!

Pat Bates was one of the longest hitters on the Buy.com Tour. I instructed Pat for quite awhile, helping him refine his swing and improve his game. One day he called to cancel his lesson because something "popped" in his neck. When his neck didn't get any better, Pat went in for surgery but something awful happened. He became partially paralyzed on his left side. Effectively, his Tour career was over.

However, Pat had a wonderful attitude and I continued to work with him over the following months on his strength, stretching, and golf swing. His persistence paid off … this year he lost in a playoff at the Buy.com Ozarks Open.

I'm really proud of Pat. Perhaps his story will motivate others to continue when it appears that the going is just too difficult.

Todd Anderson
Director of Instruction
The Breakers
Palm Beach, Fla.

PGA High Flyers

If you play at Starr Pass in Tucson, Ariz., you will have great weather and the added treat of watching some of our country's best fly to their base in US Air Force F-16 Fighting Falcons, a supersonic jet fighter plane. Well, I used to fly one of those planes and that F-16 helped me become a member of The PGA of America.

In the spring of 1985, I was a member of the 62 Fighter Squadron in Tampa, Fla., instructing students on how to fly the F-16. At golf, I was a struggling 12 handicap, but could consistently beat my boss during those Saturday morning matches. On one such Saturday, my boss informed me that I was to fly to Miami to lead a special formation of two F-16s. The second fighter would be a two-seat version and have a special passenger who was to "see everything the Falcon could do." This flight was to take place during a conference attended by what seemed like every general in the Air Force. "Why me?" I wondered, "is this because I always beat my boss at golf?" The next week I landed the formation in Miami.

As the pilot of the lead F-16, I stood by my jet to meet this mysterious VIP. As his plane landed, I noticed a big, multicolored umbrella on the tail. I had seen that logo somewhere before ... on a golf shirt from back home. Out of the plane stepped Arnold Palmer.

I had lunch that day with Mr. Palmer and led his F-16 flight the next morning. His skill at flying the Falcon was absolutely fabulous – he flew formation like a professional. Spending that time with Mr. Palmer was memorable not just because of his legendary status, but because I got to witness his class act in person. No less than 200 Air Force members lined up to have their photo taken with him and he proceeded to autograph each and every one. Later that day, we talked of careers for a fighter pilot, like me, after he stops flying. Mr. Palmer suggested I consider becoming a golf professional since I really loved the game.

I retired from the Air Force in 1991 and became a PGA member in 1994. The day after the membership interview, I sent Mr. Palmer a thank you note for his inspiration that started me on such a rewarding path. I did get one pointer from him during those few days in 1985, "Practice your short game." It still works!

Ed Britton
PGA Teaching Professional
Tucson, Ariz.

Remembering Rae Creasy

All of us who golf, at sometime or another, have competed in the name of charity. The PGA raises and donates millions of dollars each year to various organizations hoping to do their part in researching cures, combatting diseases, and helping individuals not as fortunate.

This is a story about a 14-year-old boy, Rae Creasy, who loved life and golf. Rae was born with cystic fibrosis. He struggled to survive his entire life, but his life is also a story of courage, perseverance, kindness, love, and faith. Every day was a challenge he would meet head on. He spent one hour of therapy each morning and 40 minutes every night, but his greatest therapy seemed to be golf.

Rae loved the game of golf and how it in turn could help others in need. Each August, the Pittsburgh Foundation for Cystic Fibrosis holds its annual Charity Golf Tournament. Thousands of dollars are raised to help children like Rae. Since the age of six, Rae worked at this tournament. Every year PGA Professional Joseph Sepesy, from Longue Vue Club, was instrumental in helping Rae through the tournament, giving him tips along the way. Rae will be remembered sitting there for hours in the sun, drawing the door prize tickets, with a big smile as each winner was announced. Rae loved to present the winning teams with their awards. He will be remembered for his positive attitude and enjoying the simple things in life. After getting to know Rae, our head professional, Dan Priest, at the Country Club of Ashland, began supporting events with the Cystic Fibrosis Foundation.

Rae died Nov. 5, 1998, in Pittsburgh Children's Hospital. Three months before his death, Rae played in the Cystic Fibrosis

Foundation Charity golf tournament along with his father, grandfather, and uncle. They won first place and Rae was presented with a new set of golf clubs for his efforts. Certainly, no one thought that would be Rae's last time on a golf course.

As I stood in the funeral home remembering Rae, his golf clubs, scout uniform, Indian costume, guitar, and school achievement awards, were surrounding me and each brought back wonderful memories. Rae was a hero. He loved, he shared, and lived every day as if it was his last. He was so grateful for every opportunity, especially to play in a golf tournament to benefit others with cystic fibrosis. I cannot thank The PGA of America and all their champions enough for giving young Rae the gift of life through his golf. As Rae would say, "I gave it my best shot." Through his 14 years fighting the battle of cystic fibrosis, Rae, too, was a champion.

Kyle Creasy
Ashland, Ohio

Surprise Shot

Four years ago, I was playing in a pro-am at Las Sendas Golf Club in East Mesa, Ariz. Having spent most of my life on a golf course and being a PGA Professional, I thought I had seen just about every shot possible in the game of golf. However, on this day, I witnessed the most unusual shot I had seen in 25 years of playing. The tournament format was two best balls of the fivesome, so everyone was playing very assertively.

One of our amateur players was going to play a fairway wood into the par-5, seventh hole. The seventh hole plays uphill and long and the turf was fairly moist that day due to some rain the day before our event. The golfer made a very aggressive swing but only contacted the top portion of the ball. With the upslope and soft turf, the ball was driven immediately into the ground a couple of inches, then proceeded to fly straight backwards a couple feet off the ground for a distance of about 10 feet back down the slope.

Because the ball was topped, it now had overspin, and when the ball landed it proceeded to again come back up the slope at the golfer. The golfer was jumping all over the place to get out of the way ... twice! The ball ended up about the same place it started. Being professionals, we were supposed to maintain some composure – but we were so stunned by what had occurred, that after the initial amazement, we all burst out laughing.

Jim Umbarger
PGA Apprentice
Dave Pelz Golf Schools Instructor
Pinehurst, N.C.

Tale of a Shank

A number of years ago I played in the semifinal of the Trans-Nzoia Open in Eldoret, Kenya. I shanked my 9-iron to the 17th green into the gallery of spectators and lost my match. From that moment on I became a chronic shanker under pressure and a complete neurotic on the course, frequently going sideways like a crab whenever I got near the green.

I went back to Glasgow, Scotland, for a holiday with my father, himself a 4-handicap golfer. He listened to my tale of woe and said, "I don't have any cures for shanking. Go and see old man Ballingall. He is a great teacher and his assistant is his son, Tom, one of the best golfers in Scotland."

The next day found me, not on the green sward of a golf course or a practice range, but in a large dingy room off Buchanan Street in the heart of Glasgow. Netting was draped on the walls and the professional, visibly wincing after watching me hit just two horrendous shanks with my 9-iron, suddenly shouted, "Stop! For God's sake, stop!"

He told me to make one simple adjustment to my swing and lo and behold, my shank was suddenly gone, shot after shot going straight and true. I was overjoyed and said to him, " I don't believe it, this is wonderful. It's like a miracle. How much do I owe you for the lesson?" The professional was a chubby old man sitting Tommy Armour style, like Buddha on a high chair, and he slowly got off it and came over to me. He laid his hand on my arm and patted me gently. "Laddie!" he said with a beautiful smile, "There's nae charge. The look of pleasure on yer face is payment enough." I left my lesson feeling like a new man.

What the professional had done for me was simply tell me to relax and take the club back slowly. What he taught me was to not let my own self-pressure defeat me. It is really amazing how much better a person can play if they just calm down and enjoy the game!

Dr. Lewis S. Forbes
Anza, Calif.

Shoot First, Question Later

After Labor Day in 1959, my wife and I were enjoying a few days, without our four lovely children, at magnificent North Lake Tahoe. One morning I decided to play golf at the sporty nine-hole Brockway Golf Club. I introduced myself to Betty, the pleasant lady in the golf shop, and mentioned that I was an assistant golf professional at the Lake Chabot Golf Club in Oakland, Calif. Betty was pleasant and immediately extended me the privilege to play.

On the course there was only one man waiting for a game. After no more than an exchange of names – "Dick," "Jack" – he said, "I'm a 10 handicap, how about playing for a few bucks?"

In those days, an assistant golf professional barely made enough to make ends meet. Due to this impecunious state I quite dubiously asked what he had in mind. "I'll make it easy on you. How about two bucks first, second nine and 18, with automatic press after you're two down?"

From experience, I know that a 10 is capable of shooting any kind of score. Obviously, this guy thought he had a pigeon when he saw me and knew he could play better than his 10. My "Irish," however, was piqued. So I said, "OK."

I scraped around the first nine, had five bogeys, was four over and lucky to win the ninth to break even. "You were lucky," said Jack, "How about double the bet on the next nine?"

I realized that I had played nine holes carefully, so as not to lose. I had let my indignation towards this wise guy, doubt as to my own ability, and fear of losing, take over. I was playing right into his hands; so I re-grouped.

I cleared my mind of negative thinking, concentrated on tempo, and just let the ball fly toward the target. Two holes, he was down two – press – four holes, four down – press – six holes, six down – press. He was trying to ruffle my feathers with an additional $5 bet on the remaining nine and 18. I had played the second nine with five birdies and no bogeys and he had lost every bet.

When we went into the golf shop I was feeling invigorated having just nailed this wise guy who surely thought he had found a timorous pigeon. After I told Betty how much I appreciated her courtesy she called to her husband, the club professional, "Bob, this is the fellow I was telling you about. Meet the assistant golf professional from Oakland." As I looked over at her husband, I realized it was "Jack." We just stared at each other for a moment and with a wink, I strolled out of the shop.

Richard Flynn
PGA Life Member
Oakland, Calif.

Sam Snead negotiates a trouble shot during the 1945 PGA Championship at Moraine Valley Country Club in Dayton, Ohio.

Slammin' Sam: Golf's Sweetest Swing and Briefest Lesson

Sam Snead was a self-taught player, as were two of his famed contemporaries, Byron Nelson and Ben Hogan. To be able to build your swing and use it to perfection, as he did for so many years, is truly a gift.

In 1979, I was struggling with my swing and my game. It's tough, when you're a Tour professional and you need to find a "pro's pro" who can spot the problem and help you work it out quickly. Today's Tour professionals don't have to look far for help. They can usually meet their coach, most often a PGA Professional, who can join them at a site on the tour.

My late husband, Don, knew Sam after having hunted and fished with him for several years. Don called Sam, who agreed to meet us at The Homestead in Hot Springs, Va. We got in our travel trailer and made the long trip through the mountains to find Sam.

Once we arrived, we headed to the practice range and Sam would go through his clubs and hit all kinds of shots. I would practice alongside him on the range and found myself mimicking his rhythm.

Sam had a great eye and would spot one or two things quickly, just after I had hit about four balls. His early analysis was that I was too quick off my right foot and that I appeared to be trying to kill the ball.

Sam spotted my problems fast and things began to look better. The lesson didn't last more than 30 minutes. Then, he'd say, "Let's go play."

I started 3-under-par on the front nine and ended up winning a $10 Nassau from him. He didn't like that. Sam hated to lose, but playing with him couldn't help but make you a better player.

Sam's gift was his rhythm and his control of the golf club. He never hit a short iron hard in his life. If he did, he would lose control. He had the same swing with every club.

Sam also told a jillion stories. He still has a memory like you can't believe. He remembered playing a match in 1927 in Miami.

At the end of our first lesson, Sam was hitting drives that went straight out about 230 and gently slid to the right, coming to rest at 270.

"Sam, how did you do that?" I asked in amazement. "You got that ball to take a fade at the very end of its flight!"

"Aw, you just keep the clubhead open at impact a little bit longer," he said, with a twinkle in his eyes.

I knew at that moment any hopes of copying Sam had ended. Sam Snead was a maestro with a golf club. The rest of us just tried to play his sweet music.

JoAnne Carner
Winner of Two LPGA Major Championships
Palm Beach, Fla.

The President's Professional

I have earned the distinction amongst the golfing and non-golfing public as the "President's Professional." As one writer put it during the administration of the elder George Bush as president, "He is the only golf professional who can call the White House and talk to the President in the Oval Office without secretarial interference or even hesitation."

My offhanded remark that President Bush would rather face hostile Congressional members over a controversial bill than a four-foot putt was quoted by media throughout the world in the early '90s. When I presented the president with a new long handle putter, newspapers as far away as Asia published the photograph of the president using his new putter.

Since 1979 I have been the professional at Cape Arundel Golf Club in Kennebunkport, Maine. The club was established in 1897. Walter Travis designed the course in 1921, and the Bush-Walker families have played a vital role in the history of the venerable club. President Bush's father, Senator Prescott Bush, was president of the United States Golfing Association and his maternal grandfather donated the Walker Cup for the international collegiate golfing competition.

During the four years of the Bush presidency, my face (and moustache) was known to millions of nightly news television viewers. I rode along as a passenger as the President drove the golf car at the 5,869-yard course, with a white rating of 67.0 and a slope of 117, and played the 18 holes in less than two hours.

A detachment of Secret Service agents in cars and on foot assisted President Bush and his fellow players and the White House press corps, print, and broadcast, "took over" the wide porch of the Cape Arundel clubhouse during the round.

When asked by reporters how President Bush played I would give my standard answer: "He's a good ball striker." I was pleased that the President relied heavily on my advice on how to hit a particular shot, especially if the ball was close to the green. "What do I do now, Ken?" was not an unusual question.

My expertise as a professional teacher was not only used by the President but by the former first lady, Barbara Bush. Mrs. Bush was a tennis player, but not a golfer. I gave her a series of lessons and now she plays regularly at Cape Arundel often with my wife, Anne. The day Mrs. Bush broke 100 was celebrated by the club's members, and her score almost equaled the enthusiasm displayed when professional Fred Couples, playing with the former president and myself, posted the course record of 62.

My wife, Anne, and I have enjoyed a close friendship with the President and Mrs. Bush and were guests at the White House, a thrill of a lifetime.

President Bush and I share a genuine love for the game of golf and still play together on Cape Arundel during the summer months. We also share another mutual interest – we are both ardent, dedicated fishermen. On occasion, we fish together in my skiff on the tidal Kennebunk River, next to the club or aboard President Bush's famed "Fidelity" for deep sea fishing in the Atlantic off the coast of Maine.

Many Presidents have been golfers, but no President has been closer to the game than President Bush, thanks to his family's golfing heritage. I cherish our friendship.

Ken Raynor
PGA Professional
Kennebunkport, Maine

The "Gentleman" PGA Professional

I realize that all PGA Professionals are very dedicated to the sport and to their students, but every once in awhile one seems to stand out above the rest.

When I was a senior on the St. John's University golf team, we were scheduled to play in the New York Metropolitan Intercollegiate Championships to be held that year at the Bonnie Briar Club in Larchmont, N.Y.

At the time, this was the most important golf match of my young career and none of my teammates had ever seen the course.

As luck would have it, my dad was a member of Bonnie Briar and I had met Sal DiBouno, the head professional. Sal was the ultimate gentleman. His daily dress consisted of slacks, a white dress shirt, a tie with a tie bar, and a gray fedora. You could spot Sal anywhere because he always looked like Tom Landry on game day, even when he was out on the course with a lesson.

I mentioned our tournament to Sal and asked him if we could simply walk the course on a Monday when the club was closed. Clearly he could have said, "No," but being the professional he was, he not only said, "Yes," but he said, "Better yet, why don't you and your team play the course?"

Sal was a true professional, genuinely interested in seeing golfers, and especially junior golfers, improve. I can't thank Sal enough for his kindness and all of the things he did to make me love the game to this day.

Bob Guckenberger
St. Petersburg, Fla.

A Squirrel Story

In 1974, I was the assistant professional at the Cherry Hills Country Club in Englewood, Colo., where I had been for six years. One of the fun parts of my day was feeding a squirrel that lived in a tree behind the ninth green, next to the grill and the golf shop. It loved dry roasted peanuts and soon it began to depend on its daily ration from the golf shop staff. The squirrel became so tame that it would take food right out of our hands and even come into the shop if it was not too crowded.

One morning, our squirrel was waiting for his peanuts on the window ledge just outside the golf shop and a guest was inside waiting for his partner to arrive. I thought it might be fun to show the guest just how domesticated this squirrel had become. I offered a peanut to the squirrel, holding it between the index finger and the thumb of my right hand. The squirrel took the peanut and the guest was impressed. I then shook my hand to release another peanut from my palm, which frightened the squirrel, and it bit down hard on my index finger. It wrapped its tiny paws around my hand and the tip of my index finger was halfway down its throat. It gnawed away and blood was starting to flow freely. Finally the squirrel let go, and when we could not stop the bleeding it was off to the emergency room for me.

In the hospital, I learned that squirrels were known to carry rabies and that if I did not produce the offending rodent's cranium to the medical center for testing, I would have to undergo a series of 14 very painful rabies shots. I formulated a plan.

I borrowed a 22-caliber pistol from a co-worker and the next morning I baited the squirrel with a pile of peanuts placed on the sidewalk in front of the grill room. The squirrel arrived and I squeezed off a shot which hit the squirrel and though wounded, it leapt into the air and hit the ground running. I chased the squirrel and fired another five shots, which finally stopped it. From behind a voice boomed, "Put the gun on the ground and step away from the squirrel!" I did as instructed and turned around to face two Cherry Hills police officers. They had been having coffee in the grill room and had watched the whole thing through the window. The officers confiscated the gun and I was issued a citation for "discharge of a firearm within city limits."

In front of the judge, I tried to plead self-defense but that was not one of my choices. The judge then rendered his decision "I shall dismiss this case with the recommendation to Mr. Brown that if something like this should ever happen again, and I think the odds are against it, that you allow the police to shoot the offending creature." I got out of there as quickly as I could.

Eventually the gun was returned, the rabies test on the squirrel was negative, and my finger healed. But, there is still a visible scar on my finger after some 25 years.

Stoney Brown
PGA Professional
Boise, Idaho

Free Drop Rule

My professional and I approached the first fairway sand trap on the right side of number four at the Palmbrook Country Club in Sun City, Ariz. After a pushed tee shot into this trap, I was amazed to find the ball "sitting up nicely." The problem was that, squatting over the ball, was one of our friendly coyotes that occupies the course during the winter months.

The coyote, at this time, was having a "call of nature" and was defecating directly over the golf ball. Undaunted by the presence of two dues paying members, the coyote continued to do his duty. He seemed to look right at us with a faint smile on his face. With few options available we simply waited.

Upon completion, the coyote trotted off, leaving us with the dilemma of how to play the shot. Following the example of the coyote and his "free drop" rule, I did the same. My justification for the free drop came from a seldom-used rule that very few people have heard about. It states "surely if a coyote gets a free drop on your ball in a hazard, then a dues paying member has the same privilege." My professional, however, was unable to locate this rule.

Glenn Burnett
Dodge City, Kan.

Thank You, Yellow Pages

Earlier in my career, I was the head professional at the Abington Country Club in Jenkintown, Pa. While the club and the job were absolutely fantastic, the 9-hole, par-33 golf course designed by A. W. Tillinghast would never be confused with Winged Foot or Baltusrol. Our club was located right in the middle of all of the great golf courses in the Philadelphia area.

One day, I arrived back at the golf shop after spending the morning playing in a tournament. My assistant saw me come in and said, "You'll never believe who is on the golf course." Deciding to play along, I tried to think of some famous golfer. "Michael Jordan?" I asked. "Nope." "Jack Nicklaus?" was my next answer. "No!" Figuring I would give it one more try I said, "Bob Hope?" "Yup." At that point I laughed and said, "Yeah, right." "No, really," he said, "Bob Hope is actually playing golf ... he's on the second hole right now!"

Still disbelieving, I walked out of the golf shop and over to the second hole. Sure enough, riding down the fairway was Bob Hope!

The legendary comedian was in the area to attend an armed forces dinner. Being an avid golfer, with a bit of time to kill, he decided to play some golf. So, he took out the yellow pages, looked up "golf" and since our facility started with the letter "A," we were the first place he called. Fortunately, our switchboard operator recognized him and did not send him away because he was not a member!

To top it off, after playing nine holes, Mr. Hope went into the bar and sang some old show tunes with Bill Walsh, a member at the club who was 93 years old at the time. Seeing him and Bob Hope having drinks, singing, and reminiscing about the old days, is still one of my greatest golf memories. I still have the picture I took with Mr. Hope on my desk and relish the chance to tell the story.

Our thanks to the yellow pages for providing a great day at the Abington Club.

Jim Smith
Head Professional
Talamore at Oak Terrace
Ambler, Pa.

The Jonathon Berry Story

"Let me win, but if I cannot win, let me be brave in the attempt." This is the oath all Special Olympics athletes recite before competition begins.

In November of 1998, I met Jonathon Berry, an 18-year-old athlete with Down syndrome, who qualified to participate in the World Games of 1999. Jonathon was a member of the North Carolina golf team, and for many of the athletes, it would be their first time away from home. Jonathon would be on his own and I had my doubts that he would be able to make it through the whole process.

As I worried about Jonathon, I knew we were in for some uncomfortable weather. Temperatures soared in the 100-degree range and we had no air conditioning. On our first night at Chapel Hill, shower steam from one of the rest rooms set off the fire alarm and all 2,000 residents had to be evacuated. I worried about Jonathon during evacuations because he wore a hearing aid so I put his roommate, Jeffery Neal, a gold medal winner, in charge of waking Jonathon in case of an emergency. The sight of the 6-foot-5 Jeff leading his five-foot "roomie" to safety was reassuring. They always made me smile when I saw them together.

The first two days of competition were for divisioning. Jonathon has a great swing and was placed in the men's fourth division with his score of 110.

The Duke Course is extremely difficult with many elevation changes. This meant a lot of trudging up and down in the 110 degree heat. Later that night, Jonathon looked at me and said, "I can't walk." He had tears in his eyes and was pointing at his thighs. The insides of his thighs were red and raw from the friction of walking 18 holes in the heat and humidity. We carried Jonathon into the UNC emergency room where doctors gave him a spray medication. The next morning his legs were still raw, but Jonathon wanted to play. We asked officials for a car for Jonathon but our request was denied.

Jeff Neal calculated that with his long legs it took him 10,000 steps to play the Duke Course, so it would take Jonathon 30,000 steps. That was a lot of walking, so we requested medical personnel to monitor Jonathon. The plan was to re-apply the medication every six holes. Soon he had a rather large gallery following him around. I am convinced that this show of support was a big factor in Jonathon's ability to stay in the competition. On each hole when Jonathon holed out, he turned to the crowd and tipped his cap to the applause, despite his pain. This was the day that decided who would take home the medals, but by the 12th hole Jonathon was starting to fade – in the 107-degree heat he was definitely laboring. A little later, Jonathon saw me and came over to tell me he hurt. I reminded him he only had two holes to go and to do his best. He looked at me with soulful eyes and said he would try. Jonathon hit three perfect shots on the last hole – two putts later we had another gold medal for our team. Jonathon raised his arms and the gallery roared; 30 people asked him to sign their caps.

How do you define courage and bravery? Jonathon Berry defined it in his play.

Bob Dougherty
PGA Professional
Cameron, N.C.

Working My Way Up

One day, when I was 12 years old, I was at home driving my mother nuts, so she forced my older brother to take me to the golf course as her way to get some relief. We went to Pottawatomie Park Golf Club. Nine holes only cost $1.50 and the second nine, which was a repeat of the first nine, was only 50 cents more. True to form, I drove my brother crazy that day, but I also fell in love with the game.

However, I had two obstacles to overcome; my parents felt that I quit everything I started, and that golf was expensive so they would not buy me clubs. Well, I showed them, I got an old set of free clubs from my baseball coach. Obviously, I was thrilled, I had taken care of problem one, now came problem two, how do I pay to play? This is when John Benzel, the first PGA Professional I ever met, entered my life. He gave me a job selling lemonade on the fifth tee at Pottawatomie for 60 cents an hour. The best part was I could play golf for free. My God, I was a member! I spent every penny I made in the golf shop. It was when Mr. Benzel gave me my first line of credit for a golf club that I knew I wanted to be like him, a PGA Professional.

I worked at the club for many years with different PGA members, and every one of them affected my life. Somehow, they gave me focus, taught me values, and helped me understand what a golf professional should be.

In 1972, I became an assistant golf professional at Pottawatomie Golf Course and an apprentice in The PGA of America. In 1975, I became head professional at the club, fulfilling my dream from the age of 12. If everything goes according to plan, I should be President of the Illinois PGA in two and a half more years. I hope all the PGA members who helped me along the way know that the time and effort they extended to me was worth it. Without the members of the PGA, who knows where I would be? But because of them, I always knew where I was going.

Dennis Johnsen
Head Professional
St. Charles, Ill.

Jack Grout (left) was a father figure to his prize pupil, Jack Nicklaus. They met at Scioto Country Club in Columbus, Ohio, where a 10-year-old Nicklaus was first introduced to golf by his father, Charlie Nicklaus. Young Jack and his teacher became the closest of friends. When Charlie Nicklaus died in 1970, Grout went from a father figure to a second father for the game's premier player. (Photo courtesy of the family of Bill Foley).

My Teacher, My Friend - Jack Grout

Unfortunately, it is becoming less frequent in today's society for a person to be able to look back and reflect on the positive influence a father or father figure has made on his or her childhood. We are, indeed, very fortunate if we can recall a father's hug awaiting us at every challenge, words of reinforcement to counter any failures, and a warm smile of approval to punctuate every success. To be able to say you had two such father figures in your life is to say you are blessed. I, then, was blessed – blessed to have had my life touched by my own dad *and* by Jack Grout.

Not only did my father offer me all the unconditional love and support a small boy could want or need, he provided the guiding hand in every sport or path I wanted to pursue. When at age 10 I first picked up a golf club and soon realized this was a path I wanted to follow, my father embraced the idea and helped me to build a firm foundation in the sport. Soon after, I met Jack Grout and he built the framework to go atop this foundation. As I said, I took up golf at age 10, when I served as my father's tag-along caddie during rounds at Scioto Country Club in Columbus, Ohio. As if destiny wanted to play a key role in my career story, Jack Grout came to Scioto as the club professional about the same time I was introduced to the game.

Born in Oklahoma and raised in Texas, Jack was the product of a golfing family. When he turned professional in October 1929, Jack worked for his older brother at a Fort Worth, Texas, club. Even his sister was a state amateur champion in Oklahoma. Jack certainly had the pedigree and the credentials; he also had the wonderful stories that seemed as valuable in his profession as a lengthy résumé. When Jack worked for his brother in Fort Worth, he would sneak off after hours to play rounds with a couple of former caddies by the names of Ben Hogan and Byron Nelson. Stories have been told that Byron and Jack partnered to win so many pro-ams, the professionals huddled and re-wrote the rules to separate the two as often as possible. Jack had a few meaningful victories to his credit, but nothing that earned him enough acclaim or financial security to deter him from his career as a teaching professional. Years of competing, and studying the game and the game's best, gave him a talent for teaching. Jack was very comfortable around people, and he had a passion for introducing the game to young people. Everyone, especially me, was the luckier for it.

In 1950, I was just one of some 50 boys and girls in Jack's summer class. But it wasn't long before you'd hear Jack call me out from the group: "Jackie boy, come here and show them how to do it." Group sessions soon turned into individual lessons, and I could not get enough of the one-on-one attention. I remember days when Jack would just stand there, grab my head by the hair, and make me hit balls like that for an hour to keep my head still. Thank goodness, I had short hair then; if I didn't, I soon would have after those lessons.

For every minute Jack and I spent studying a swing thought, there were as many hours spent just talking. Golf is a game that can teach life lessons, and Jack Grout and I spent countless and priceless hours just talking about life. It wasn't until later in my life that I realized just how special and deep was the bond Jack and I shared. When my father passed away in 1970, Jack Grout went from being a father figure in my life to a second father to me.

Golf, and many sports for that matter, are exercises in mental strength. The needle bounces up and down with our emotions. We suffer many more lows than we do highs, and one's success is sometimes predicated by how we deal with those swings and our ability to perform in that middle ground. Perhaps too often a coach or teacher's impact on this particular area of a young life is taken for granted, when in reality, there could be no greater contribution. That was the case with Jack Grout. From the day I lined up with 50 other children on the practice range at Scioto to that sad day in May of 1989 when Jack died, he touched my life in a special way like no one else had or has since.

Perhaps that is why there are certain words from Jack that have burned their place in my heart and my memories, such as the following excerpt from a letter he wrote me less than a year before his death – a letter to congratulate me for a "Golfer of the Century" honor:

> "I think I know how you did it, Jack. I used to think that the greatest thing in the world was high achievement in sport. Now that I have more time to sit around and think about things, I have decided that even greater than high achievement in sport is high achievement in sportsmanship. Your dad and your mother taught you about the second one, and I think that's why you won."

Yes, but there were also a few good lessons from you, my friend.

Jack Nicklaus
Winner of 18 Major Championships
1983, 1987 U.S. Ryder Captain
North Palm Beach, Fla.

Yes, You Can!

In 1973, Dennis Walters returned home to New Jersey after competing successfully in professional tournaments on the South African Golf Tour. His lifelong dream was to play the PGA Tour and he had an excellent chance to become certified at the PGA Tour Qualifying School to be played the following month. Anxious to see his friends, Dennis drove a three-wheeled golf car across a hilly, New Jersey course to meet them. He lost control of the car. It rolled over a bank and landed on his legs. Within a few days, he was told that he would never walk again.

The use of his lower body was taken away but the one thing that couldn't be taken was his love of golf. Dennis was hitting golf balls from a wheel chair within several months of the accident. Soon thereafter, an inventive friend developed a swiveling seat that could be attached to a golf car. Strapping himself into it, he could hit golf balls with stability. Hitting golf balls added so much to his life and people loved watching him.

But what would he do with his life? His dreams were shattered. His mobility was reduced to a wheelchair, his mind in turmoil.

That was 27 years ago. Since that time, Dennis Walters has won several national golf awards, including the prestigious Ben Hogan Award in 1978 for the Comeback Golfer of the Year, and is one of only a few honorary members of The PGA of America. He has entertained United States presidents and proudly displays their personal letters in his home. He has performed with golf's greatest players and is a friend to the likes of Arnold Palmer, Jack Nicklaus, and the late Ben Hogan. For the past three years, he has been Tiger Woods' opening act at all of Tiger's junior clinics across the US. He has a schedule of approximately 100 shows a year from Florida to California. Dennis Walters, with the help and love of his family (and trusty dog, Benji Hogan), has become a great success. And, as he says, "If I could do it, so could you!"

Dennis does a motivational golf trick shot show where he displays a mastery of golf and inspiration. The consistency of his shots impresses even the world's greatest players. It is truly amazing how he hits accurate shots with clubs ranging from drivers to putters; clubs with fishing pole shafts to shafts with four hinges; club-heads made from a judge's gavel to a cellular phone. Every shot is hit with a slight draw; every shot is hit down the middle.

His motivation leaves you speechless as he tells you that he is going to give, "Golf lessons as well as life lessons." His life lesson is that if he could make it so could you. And Dennis Walters has made it.

A long list could be compiled of the numerous TV shows on which he has appeared. Magazine and newspaper articles are in the thousands. Virtually every player on the PGA, LPGA, and Senior Tour knows the name Dennis Walters, but that's not what keeps him going. What keeps him going is his message; "There are very few things in the world that are impossible to do. If you have a dream and if you work hard, you could achieve almost anything."

This simple, yet profound message has influenced people at each of his thousands of shows over the past 20 years. Even if Dennis had become a number one player on the PGA Tour, he wouldn't have compiled half of the triumphs, victories, or successes that he has achieved. Dennis Walters has changed people's lives. He has inspired individuals of all ages and from all walks of life from his living example, "YES, YOU CAN!"

Jay Golden
PGA Golf Clinician
Winter Park, Fla.

Jack Doss, an Unforgettable PGA Professional

It's been a little over eight years since I took up the game of golf. When I started, my friend, Doug, a more experienced golfer, who was probably tired of seeing me slice every ball, politely suggested that I seek instruction from an excellent PGA Professional he knew named Jack Doss. I decided to accept his advice and the call to Jack changed my golfing life for the better and earned me a treasured friendship with one of the warmest human beings I've ever known.

For one reason or another, I hadn't taken golf lessons before and as I drove down the palm tree-lined lane into the Santa Clara Golf and Tennis facility, I was a bit nervous. I tried to envision what this strange new experience of a golf lesson might be like. There, at the first mat on the practice range, flanked by his ever-present video camera, was the man who would eventually be responsible for lowering my score from 110 to 80.

From a distance, he reminded me of the actor, Buddy Ebsen, from the *Barnaby Jones* television series. He had the same graying light brown hair, 6-foot tall medium frame, and handsome sun-and-wind tinged face. As I approached, his warm smile was already putting me at ease. I remember saying, "I'm a beginner."

Within the first 10 minutes, Jack remedied my slice by having me add another knuckle's worth of strength to my left-hand grip. Most importantly, he enabled me to feel, for the first time, that wondrous sensation of hitting down on the ball. He accomplished this task by methodically positioning my arms, shoulders, and hips as he led me through the swing, ending it with his trademark drill: him gripping the shaft about one-third of the way from the bottom and forcing me to thump the mat while missing the ball on the inside in front of the ball. I remember in countless subsequent lessons, Jack would say,

"Take your grip and hold on real good." He would then lead me through those increasingly familiar positions and have me thump the mat. "That's a good feeling for you," he'd impart.

My lessons with Jack always involved drills and various items that he would position in and around the mat to force me to make a proper swing and to ultimately hit down on the ball. "Hit it on the doon swing," he'd say, in his best imitation of a Scottish brogue. I'd have to miss the penny or the clipboard he'd placed behind my ball. Or, I'd have to avoid the bucket, the rubber tubing, or a myriad of other props that Jack creatively incorporated. He is the master of getting his student to feel the requisite motions and positions.

As I reflect on my lessons with Jack, I feel like *Kung Fu's* "Grass Hopper" who was always hearing his master's voice giving him counsel. There are probably a dozen swing thoughts instilled in me by Jack that will never leave my memory banks.

Once, I had fallen into a bad habit of dropping my right shoulder and consequently coming out of my swing as I brought the club down. A man named Roger was sitting in a white chair a few yards behind us, observing the lesson. Jack told me to, "Look at Roger" as I was about to make impact. That helped me considerably. I became a madman over the next few improved rounds. I'm sure others in my foursome could hear me muttering that phrase to myself like some kind of mystical incantation every time I stood on the tee-box.

My all-time favorite swing thought, however, is the "battering ram." I never could figure out how to initiate and proceed through the appropriate positions once I had the club cocked and poised for action at the top of my back swing. Jack explained that everything happens way too fast (about 1.3 seconds), so there was no time for me to think of such things. He took me over to a nearby pole and had me tap it with the butt of my club handle as I moved the club into the impact position. "It's like a battering ram," Jack told me. I absolutely annihilated the ball after that. The difference was incredible! It totally cured the miry slump I had fallen into. Feeling like a parched man that had finally been led to an oasis, I looked at Jack and asked, "Why didn't you teach me that sooner?"

The man has such a wellspring of knowledge. I could take lessons forever and probably not begin to exhaust it. Actually, this shouldn't be surprising. Jack was a money winning tour player back during the era in which Arnold Palmer played. After that, he served as a club professional under former Master's champion, Claude Harmon, at the famed Winged Foot Golf Club. He has set several course records (his 63 still stands as the record at Baton Rouge Country Club). And, as an instructor, he has flourished even more – he was named 1997 Teacher of the Year by the Northern California Section of The PGA of America.

The single most memorable experience I've had with Jack occurred during a practice round.

Jack and I teed off on the back nine and I got off the tee in lackluster fashion, while Jack hit a prodigious drive with his brand new graphite-shafted titanium Great Big Bertha Driver. I complimented him on his drive and he began enthusiastically telling me all the new driver's specifications and how this exceptional new club was performing better than any other he had hit to date. He was really proud of this club.

Several double bogeys into the round, it became glaringly clear that I had fallen into a horrendous mode of coming over the top on every swing. I simply couldn't stop doing it. Jack had a sudden flash of insight as to how to alleviate this malady. Recall that one of Jack's favorite teaching techniques is to use props with which to force the student to make a correct swing path. He instructed me to set up to my target and prepare to swing while he gripped the head of his driver and positioned the shaft parallel to my target line about 3 feet away from my body. Now I was assured of making a proper swing. I went through my usual waggles and glances at the target, and then took the best swing I knew on my 4-iron. As I brought my club into the downswing, something went wrong. Rather than a solid impact with the ball, I had a solid impact with Jack's club. I immediately glanced back at Jack quizzically as I've done a hundred times before to get his analysis of what went wrong and there, on the fairway, was the shaft of his brand new great Big Bertha Driver. It was chopped perfectly in half by my 4-iron.

My profuse apologies didn't even matter, as Jack didn't skip a beat. He indicated that it wasn't my fault and it may not have been one of his better ideas for curing a swing problem. Although somewhat shell shocked, we continued the playing lesson.

Over the years that followed, Jack and I would occasionally joke about the incident, but mainly we focused on making improvements to my golf swing, which Jack has done admirably. He has become more than my teacher and golfing guru. Jack is a friend whose warmth will stay in my heart and whose words I will hear in my head each time I make a golf swing.

Rick Knoblaugh
Groveland, Calif.

Harry Pezzullo (right), the golf professional of the stars, gives a tip to Mickey Wright during the 1970s at Mission Hills Country Club in Chicago. Wright, perhaps the greatest woman golfer in history, was one of many who sought Pezzullo's advice.

Mobsters at Midnight

It was in the mid-1960s and I was at home on this July night smoking my pipe and in pajamas watching the Friday Night Fights sponsored by Gillette. The kids were still up and playing in the living room when the telephone rang about 11 o'clock. My wife answered the phone. "It's for you," she said. "It's some man with a deep voice."

The voice at the end of the line said, "Hey, it's Sam. Come down and give me golf lessons."

"Come down where?" I asked, incredulously.

"To your range at your club."

I said, "Wait a minute. Hey, you've got be crazy. We don't have any lights."

"Don't worry about the lights," said Sam Giancanna. "We've got lights."

I looked at my wife and said, "OK," and hung up the phone.

"You'd better do something," my wife said. "I'm not going to have those guys come over here and bother these kids."

I put my slacks on. It was a hot night in July. It took me about 20 minutes to get to the course, Mission Hills Country Club. I arrived in the parking lot and found seven black Cadillacs and one Ford Cessna. Sam always drove the Ford. They always played at the club two or three days a week. Every time they came in they paid for everything with cash. They would buy a dozen balls apiece.

Sam said he had lost $600 earlier that day playing golf. He and his pals would get into two foursomes. I looked on the ground and saw a whole box – 144 new balls. Sam was wearing a tan silk shirt and a tie. They were going downtown to watch a show at the Chez Paris nightclub where Eddie Fisher, Dean Martin and Sammy Davis Jr. were playing. Frank Sinatra was in town, but wasn't performing that night.

We started the lesson. The first thing I noticed was that Sam's grip was wrong. His left hand was strangling the club. I put his right hand around to settle comfortably on the club into a proper grip. Then, Sam started off with some irons.

After he had hit a few, he told an associate to go out and pick up the balls. He had a picker-upper with him, but immediately complained, "I can't go out there. You'll hit me with the ball!"

Sam said, "OK, never mind. I'll hit some and then we'll pick them up."

After he hit about 95 balls, a couple of us went out and got them. We picked up what we could see.

So now, with the lesson over, Sam said that he felt better. "I'm tired. But I've got it. You've straightened me out."

He reached into his pocket and handed me a bill. It was dark, and I just thought it was a $100, and put it in my pocket.

"You cheap, SOB," he said, "You think I come out here at midnight to get a lesson for $100?" He grabbed me by the neck. "You give me my change!"

I reached into my pocket and saw that it was a $1,000 bill. I was shocked. "OK. I'll get your change from the clubhouse."

I went to the safe and got ten $100 bills. I brought them out and Sam looked and one of his guys started counting. Then, Sam gave me $300.

Sam went to his car to change his shirt. He couldn't get his tie off it was so wet with perspiration. He asked someone for a knife, so, some guy cut his tie off. Sam opened his trunk and found a new tie. He also had extra shirts and a couple of sportcoats.

"I'll see you tomorrow," said Sam.

In the morning, I went back out and found about 40 or 50 new balls and cleaned them up and put them on the counter and sold them for a dollar apiece.

I saw Sam and his group playing around 10 in the morning. I later learned he won $500 or $600. He began to win each time after that. He'd send some of his friends to me for lessons. He treated me like one of them and we never had any trouble. You know why?

We never let on to anyone, especially the media, who was playing three times a week on our course.

Harry Pezzullo
PGA Life Member & Head Professional Emeritus
BallenIsles Country Club
Palm Beach Gardens, Fla.

You Must Have Read It Wrong!

It was the kind of day every amateur golfer dreams about ... bright sunshine at The National Car Rental Golf Classic at Walt Disney World. For several years, I've had the good fortune to play in the pro-am portion of this event – an unusual format in which the amateurs actually play Thursday and Friday, the first two days of the official tournament, paired with a different professional each day, in a foursome with another pro-am team.

This year, for my opening round, I drew a young professional named Tom Scherrer who, with a win at the Kemper Open, was wrapping up his best year on the tour. The other professional in our foursome was Chris DiMarco, who would finish the year in the top 30 money winners and go on to play in the Tour Championship.

It was a bright, breezy fall day in Florida as we teed off on Disney's Magnolia Course. I hit an OK drive, pushed an iron, and followed that with a mediocre bunker shot leaving me with a very fast 30-footer for par.

Since these rounds are "work days" for the professionals, I try to stay out of their way as best I can. Nevertheless, I'm amazed how friendly they can often be, sometimes helping their amateur partners with their swings or reading putts. That day was no exception and I quickly realized that Tom and Chris were as nice a couple of guys as you'd ever want to play with. Although he put his opening drive into an unplayable lie and was looking at a bogey, Tom put his own problems aside, and walked over to read my 30-foot putt. I accepted Tom's assessment of the break and now without the line to worry about, I hit it pure ... speed just right, dead center for net birdie ... it was an omen.

From tee to green, my game was as ragged as ever, but my putting entered that "zone" I had often heard the professionals talk about. With Tom giving me the line, it seemed as if I could make every putt. The second hole was a hard breaking eight-footer. The fourth hole was a slippery 10-footer. The sixth hole was 20 feet, if it was an inch. The eighth hole was a 15-footer with the added pressure of a large gallery.

By the turn, both Professionals were commenting on my putting. On any other occasion, such compliments would have been the "kiss of death," but that day the magic continued. With Tom giving me the line, all I had to do was get the speed right. The 10th hole was another 8-footer. The 12th hole, I missed the green, flubbed a chip, then drained a 30-footer from the fringe.

The 17th at Magnolia is a long dogleg-left, par-4 with water left on the drive and right on the approach. Three ugly shots after teeing off found me on the back of the green with my longest putt of the day – a full 40-feet, downhill, big break towards the pond – but once again, Tom, who was nearing the end of a forgettable round, walked over to read my putt. This time he really had his work cut out for him. He studied the break and then established my line with great confidence.

Once again, I stroked it pure. Good speed, took the break perfectly, looking good … the ball caught the hole, dove in, but then went 360 degrees and came out again. There was a moment of total silence until we all realized it wasn't going to drop.

Then, from across the green, and in a voice loud enough for the entire gallery to hear, Chris turned to Tom and announced with a shrug, "Well, obviously you read it wrong!"

Michael Lollis
Atlanta, Ga.

The Perfect Lesson in Bunker Play

At the National Open in 1961, at Oakland Hills Country Club, in Bloomfield Hills, Mich., three golfing buddies and I received access to attend the Tuesday morning practice round. We wanted to follow Arnold Palmer and actually see as many of the best players as possible without tournament pressure. We were walking in a group of about 10 with Arnie's foursome at the third hole. Just after all the players had hit their drives, one of them offered a substantial bet on who would be closest to the hole after their second shot. All the players agreed. Unfortunately, Arnie hit his second into the bunker on the right of the green. He then proceeded to miss his bunker shot, but rather than moving on, he turned to us and said, "There's no reason to miss a sand shot like this that badly." He took out six balls and placed them in a line in the trap. Then gave us a perfect lesson in bunker play from set up to club face and swing. He just walked through the six balls he had just dropped, hitting each exactly the same without looking up. He then mentioned that usually it's better to be in a bunker than the rough or fringe because sand is controllable, deep grass isn't. When we looked up, all six of his lesson shots were within 18 inches of the hole. I learned a great lesson from a great golfer that day and have admired Arnold Palmer ever since for his attitude, interest and concern.

Gerald Richardson
Parsippany, N.J.

If You Can't Beat Them, Join Them

Golf is a funny game and it can sometimes put stress on a relationship between a husband and a wife. You can't play on a weekend, anywhere, without giving up about six hours of quality time with your family. It takes time to get to the club, time to warm up, four hours on the course, time to shower, have a beer, and time to get home … six hours, minimum.

Well, under the theory "If you can't beat them, join them," I decided I'd try to get my wife, Mary, involved in the game. One day, I took her to the practice range at Calumet Country Club in Homewood, Ill. I encouraged her to just swing a club and to get the feel of chipping a few balls on the practice green. She tried, but with little success.

As I stood there watching her futile efforts to chip the ball, our head professional, Randy Wexter, passed by. He saw our frustration and offered to help my wife with a 20 minute impromptu lesson. He fixed her grip and in a short while had her chipping quite well.

Today, Mary is the Chairperson of her Ladies' Nine-Hole League. More importantly, she has developed a passion for the game and we totally enjoy playing together on weekends and vacations.

I honestly don't think this would have occurred if Randy Wexter had not gone out of his way to assist a new golfer.

In my opinion, Randy is what I think *A Spirit of Golf* is all about.

Bernard D. Greenawalt
Tinley Park, Ill.

Claude Harmon at His Best

Lanny Wadkins often went to Butch Harmon for help with his game. On one occasion, his father, Claude Harmon, joined them for a playing lesson. After watching Wadkins hit a perfect 3-wood off a downhill lie to a green fronted by a pond, Claude turned to Butch and asked, "Tell me, son. Just what do you plan to teach this young man?"

Following the round, Wadkins asked the 1948 Masters Champion if he had any advice.

"Lanny, just make sure you vary your route to the bank," the elder Harmon replied.

* * * * *

Butch Harmon is well known as Tiger Woods' teacher, but several years ago he gained attention for his work with Greg Norman. Working with high-profile tour professionals didn't impress Harmon's father, Claude, all that much, however.

"Hell, Butch," the former head professional at Winged Foot and Seminole told his son, "anyone can teach Greg Norman. He's already one of the best players in the world. The real challenge is teaching a bunch of your members who can barely get the ball into the air. That's where the real fun is."

* * * * *

The late Dave Marr, who won the 1965 PGA Championship, worked as an assistant professional under Claude Harmon at Winged Foot, and always gave Harmon a great deal of credit for his success.

"Claude had a trick that he sometimes used with his assistants, especially if we were getting ready to play in a tournament," said Marr. "If he thought you were getting too mechanical, he'd take half the clubs out of your bag and then send you out to play. It forced you to hit creative shots and figure out a way to get the ball into the hole using non-tradition methods and finesse. It was a great teaching lesson."

Don Wade
Editorial Director – Golf Society of the U.S.
Stamford, Conn.

From Russia, with Love of the Game

In 1989, I was contacted by Swen Tuba, a golf professional, who first made his name in the Olympics for his native Sweden. Swen asked for my help with an ambitious project. He had been hired to build Russia's first golf course, a nine-hole facility in Moscow. Further, Russia wanted to become more involved in golf and they had selected their 15 best students for an extensive training program in America. The hope was that those 15 students would return to Russia and become their country's first golf professionals, teaching other kids who would then go through the youth golf training program.

I was fortunate to be one of the PGA Professionals selected to work with these fine Russian youths while they were in America. They visited me at The Falls Country Club in Lake Worth, Fla., and spent three days observing and experiencing actual hands-on work in all facets of golf course maintenance, golf shop management, and teaching and playing techniques.

I showed them how the greens were mowed and we spent one day with our maintenance department going through how a golf course is prepared for a day's play. Each student was even allowed to experience mowing a green and a fairway.

I spent one day working with them on teaching and swing technique and gave each of them an individual private teaching lesson. Then, on the third day, we went out on the golf course and played a round in a playing lesson to learn course and game management.

They were a great group of talented young people, polite and well-mannered. Russia had sent two chaperones and an interpreter with the students, although all of the students spoke English fairly well.

When it was time for the group to return to Russia, one of the young girls, Anastasia Merezhro, wanted to stay and learn more about golf in America. We made arrangements for her to stay in our home for an additional six months, and she assisted me in the golf shop, played other courses in the area and continued working on her golf game until it was time for her to return home.

At the time, Anastasia was 16 years old, and played golf as purely and beautifully as her famous first name from the era of the czars. And, she said things that were just as sweet.

"On the golf course, people are Russians or Americans or anything else. We are just people who share a love for this game," she said. "This game transcends all international barriers, but how am I going to hit the ball out of the snow when I go home to Russia?"

I really enjoyed having this young woman with my family and knew that she would take back some special lessons to her homeland. When she left, she paid me a big compliment.

"Blue jeans are like gold in Russia," she said. "But a swing like yours is pure platinum. If I could teach golf the way you do and sell blue jeans in my country, I could buy Moscow."

Jimmy Wright
PGA Professional
Sarasota, Fla.

Water Hazard

In 1934 an 11-year-old caddie named Floyd got to caddie for Mr. Chadwick, the course owner at Boston Hills Golf Club. Mr. Chadwick was a fine golfer but also had quite a temper.

It seemed that it was a good day for Mr. Chadwick as he was 4-under-par when he reached the normally easy 16th. Teeing off from the high tee above the 180-yard across pond and dogleg right, par-4, Mr. Chadwick popped his tee shot up and his ball fell into the pond. His second tee shot went off the tip of his driver also entering the water. His frustration was so great that he threw his driver into the pond! Using a spoon for his third tee shot, he again popped it high and it also failed to clear the pond … then again, neither did the spoon. He threw it in, too.

Now follows the meat of the story. Floyd was standing by the tee with the bag and remaining clubs, struggling to hold them. Mr. Chadwick grabbed the remaining clubs and threw them, the bag, and Floyd still trying to hold on, off the tee and down into the pond.

Mr. Chadwick stomped back to the clubhouse leaving Floyd, his caddie, in the pond. Some time had passed when Floyd finally returned to the clubhouse with Mr. Chadwick's clubs and bag which he had carefully retrieved.

Mr. Chadwick, now having calmed down and having re-evaluated his behavior, reached into his pocket and handed Floyd a $100 bill. In 1934, $100 was an enormous amount of money. An embarrassed Mr. Chadwick apologized over and over.

When Floyd recovered from seeing the largest sum of money he had ever seen having been assured he should accept it, his classic statement to Mr. Chadwick went like this: "That's OK, Mr. Chadwick ... whenever you'd like to do that again, I'm your boy, just ask for Floyd."

Larry Shute
PGA Life Member
River Run Golf Club
Crossville, Tenn.

PGA Life Member Don Collett (right), former president of the World Golf Hall of Fame in Pinehurst, N.C., presents a scrapbook to President Gerald R. Ford in December 1974. Three months earlier, Collett was alongside and played golf with the 38th President of the United States, who dedicated the Hall of Fame. (Photo courtesy of The Office of Gerald R. Ford & Don Collett).

A Day with the President in Pinehurst

The date Sept. 11, 1974, may not hold special significance in the unfolding drama of the 20th century, but for many of us living in Pinehurst, N.C., it was an unforgettable day.

Newly appointed President Gerald R. Ford, who had been sworn into office just 30 days earlier following the resignation of Richard Nixon, was coming to Pinehurst to dedicate the World Golf Hall of Fame. He would be joined by eight living inductees of the original class of 13. It was, without question, the greatest array of golf talent ever assembled at one time on planet Earth.

Ben Hogan gazed skyward in disbelief as members of the Army's Golden Knights from nearby Fort Bragg put on a spectacular opening show. The paratroopers made pinpoint landings a few yards in front of the Hall honorees, which included Byron Nelson, Arnold Palmer, Gary Player, Sam Snead, Patty Berg and Jack Nicklaus.

"Unbelievable," said Nelson, squinting up into the mid-afternoon sun.

As a PGA Professional, the president of the World Golf Hall of Fame and president of the 10,000-acre Pinehurst Resort & Country Club, it *was* a very special day. I thought to myself how nice it would be to freeze the historic moment so we all could enjoy it a little longer.

When President Ford arrived to the familiar strains of "Hail to the Chief," the Hall of Fame moment capped nearly three years of planning and its expected equal portions of frustration. Ford's visit was nearly cancelled twice – the first time due to pressing matters in Washington and the second due to a threat on his life just days before he was to arrive. But here he was, and later declaring, "I wouldn't have missed it for the world."

The New York Times later tabbed the afternoon "the coup of the year." Two days after Ford had assumed office, one of his aides, Bob Goodwin, called me to cancel the President's visit. I was about to hang up when I tried a mulligan.

I told Goodwin that if the president would reconsider that I would arrange for him to play a few holes with all of the living Hall of Famers.

"Who are they?" Goodwin asked. Even though I wasn't sure I could pull this golf date off, I ticked off names like Palmer, Nicklaus, Hogan, Snead, Nelson, Player, Sarazen and Berg. Goodwin sounded unimpressed.

"Well," he said, "I'll check with the president and get back with you." A day later, I received another call from the White House asking me for a detailed schedule of events for the dedication.

A day or two passed and there was another call from the White House. This time, Goodwin asked if Ben Hogan was really going to attend. I said emphatically that he would.

"That's great. The president wants you to know he will be there, too," said Goodwin.

One by one, the Hall of Famers gave stirring, inspirational acceptance speeches. Ben Hogan told a large crowd how he and Byron Nelson had grown up in the same caddie ranks in Fort Worth, and how he won his first tournament after years of frustration and struggling in Pinehurst, of all places, in the old North and South Open.

"Thirty-four years later," said Hogan, "I have been inducted into the Hall of Fame." There wasn't a dry eye following Hogan's remarks.

Later in the ceremony, Gary Player said he would be a "bit worried if I was an American, having my president play so well." And he evoked a large roar when he murmured, "Not too much time in the office, I guess!"

Earlier that day, President Ford had hit a smashing drive on the first hole on Pinehurst No. 2, bettering the tee shots of Palmer, Player and Deane Beman, then the PGA Tour commissioner. Only Nicklaus's tee shot skipped past Ford's – by a scant five yards.

What made the tee shot more amazing was President Ford was using borrowed clubs that were delivered that day. I was a long-time member of the Ben Hogan professional staff at the time, and called Mr. Hogan at his factory in Fort Worth. I asked if he could make up a bag and set of clubs for the president to use that day.

The clubs were waiting for President Ford on the first tee. But, the cellophane wrappers had not been pulled off the clubs when the president reached for the driver. Hogan even reached to get one of the wrappers off.

President Ford made a couple of hurried practice swings, teed his ball and hit a high-arching drive down the middle of the fairway. Later in the round, Hogan stepped from the golf car to give the president instruction on how the left side should initiate the downswing. Classic instruction from a classic teacher and it was all captured on film. I even played three holes with the president and the Hall of Famers that day.

After the round, something even more remarkable happened to me.

I spent 20 minutes alone with the president in a storage area in the men's locker room that had been refurbished for the president and his aides.

But, as I stepped aside to let the president and his entourage enter, he told me to go ahead. He then closed the door and we both sat down.

"Shouldn't we let some of your friends and staff in here?" I asked awkwardly.

"Oh, no," the president said nonchalantly. "They can wait."

We drank a couple of sodas and laughed and talked about the day. The president was especially curious about the Hall of Fame and how I was able to raise the money to build it and acquire the collection of golf artifacts. He asked me about my life as a PGA Professional and how I got started in the game. He also asked about my family; especially my five sons, Randy, Rodney, Craig, Paul and Brian, all excellent players. Rodney, Paul and Brian also took turns caddying for President Ford that day. At that time, Randy was the head professional at Pinehurst; Rodney went on to become a journalist; Craig a golf course superintendent and Paul and Brian PGA Professionals.

Soon, there was a knock at the door and Bob Goodwin appeared.

"It's time to go, Mr. President."

We all would be heading to a Hall of Fame dinner that evening. We had the president of the United States on the grounds for more than eight hours.

The president later invited my wife, Verla, and I to the White House, where on Dec. 21, 1974, I presented him with a scrapbook entitled, "A Day with The President in Pinehurst." It was a fitting conclusion to the most exciting time of my life.

Donald C. Collett
PGA Life Member
San Diego, Calif.

(Editor's Note: Don Collett, a 41-year member of The PGA of America, did a feasibility study in 1971 that created the original World Golf Hall of Fame in Pinehurst, N.C. He presided over 43 inductions during his seven-year term as president; resigning in 1979 after the Hall was granted foundation status. The PGA of America assumed control of the Hall of Fame Foundation in 1981 and its contents were transferred in 1998 to today's World Golf Village near St. Augustine, Fla.)

Growing Up with Uncle Bill

Growing up the son of a PGA Tour hopeful was great, but if you love the game of golf, it was even better if he became the director of golf at the Fountainbleau Country Club when you were only 6 years old.

But what made it even more interesting was growing up around "Wild" Bill Mehlhorn. You see, he and my father, Sal Monte, developed a relationship before I was born. When dad left the tour and went to the Fountainbleau, Mr. Mehlhorn could be found there every day. I grew up calling him "Uncle Bill."

At first I just thought he was some old fellow that I had to show respect for. He'd always watch me hit balls and take me out on the golf course and hit shots with me. Mind you in 1970, Bill was 72, past his prime, but I can never remember him missing a shot.

As Uncle Bill got older and I became a teenager I began to realize who he was. He'd never brag about his past, so my only reference was what I heard and read. When sportswriters would come to the club to interview him, or the phone would ring and someone named "Ben Hogan" would be on the other end of the line asking for Mr. Mehlhorn, it all sank in.

I didn't realize just how lucky I was to be around such a champion and such a great man. He won more than 21 Tour events, played on the first Ryder Cup Team in 1927, competed in the first Masters in 1934, invented the numerical labeling system for clubs, and was someone whom Hogan labeled, "The best ball striker I have ever seen."

Bill gave me so much as a player and a teacher, but what impressed me most about this humble champion was his deep respect for all people and his amazing integrity. He lived and played by the rules, and no matter who you were, a mayor, or laborer, if you broke the rules on or off the golf course, he gave you a stern talking to.

All of his life, everyone counted with Uncle Bill. This wasn't some new personality trait he developed as he got older. In the 1920s, playing in England, professionals weren't allowed in the clubhouse. He was going through his routine with the boys, brown bagging and changing cloths in a pitched tent, when he noticed Walter Hagen missing. "Where's Walter?" "He's having lunch with the Prince of Wales in the clubhouse."

It was virtually unheard of for professionals of that era to dine inside. Uncle Bill went in to investigate. The "bobby" guarding the door stopped him. "Can't come in here, Mehlhorn." "It's 'Mr. Mehlhorn' or 'Bill' to you, now get outta my way before I knock you over."

The guard backed away and Bill walked over to Mr. Hagen and the prince. The prince invited him to join the lunch. Staring right at Hagen he said, "Nothing doing, I'm eating with my fellow professionals on the lawn!" From that day on all professionals were permitted to eat and change inside the club.

I remember his routine so very well. About 8:30 a.m., he'd pull in to the club, and immediately start shaking a box of cat food. The cats would come running. Then, he'd feed the ducks, look at the birds, walk into the coffee shop, take off his giant Stetson, pour a cup of coffee and begin a game of solitaire. I'd walk over and he'd say, "Whatta ya' know, cowboy?"

I would try to impress him with my previous days round of 37 on the front nine, which played 3,500 yards from the white tees and he'd say, "Maybe today you'll shoot a 34." I was only 11 years old!

Regretfully for me, Bill Mehlhorn passed on in 1989 at the age of 91. He left much besides his wisdom concerning golf. He taught me that we're all here sharing the earth and regardless of what you achieve, don't ever act like you're above anyone.

Uncle Bill, I'll always miss you and think of you with fond memories. Thanks.

Mike Mangiaracina
PGA Professional
The Mike Mangiaracina Academy of Golf
Indian Head Golf Park
Kings Park, N.Y.

Boxer Turned Golfer

When we got married, my husband, Alexander, was a boxer. He loved boxing … and it was his *only* hobby. He entered many competitions and he won quite a few of them. But night after night he would come home with bruises and sometimes even broken bones. I hated it and I worried about him all the time. In fact, everyone in the family worried about him.

My brother, John, played golf and he was always trying to get Alexander to play with him. But Alexander wasn't buying it. "Golf just isn't physical enough," he would say. However, one day John asked Alex to go to lunch at the golf club with him and our older brother, Richard, who had flown in from California for a visit. Over lunch, John convinced Alexander to play in a threesome that afternoon with Richard.

John is a left-handed golfer and since Alexander didn't have any clubs, Richard let him borrow his right-handed clubs. The round was a harrowing experience for Richard because both Alexander and John are practical jokers and all afternoon they terrorized him. One of the stories they told me afterwards was quite funny, involving a $500 wood that Richard owned.

Alexander had hit his shot into the rough and had taken the $500 club over to his shot. Richard had gone ahead to his shot and John was with Alex. Alex's shot had landed on the cart path, so John told him to take it off the gravel and put it on the grass, which he did, and then Alex took his swing. But John wasn't through harassing his older brother just yet, so he yelled, "Next time take it *off* the gravel!" Richard came hurrying over, concerned. "He hit it on the gravel? That's a $500 club!" John and Alexander were laughing so hard they were barely able to tell him that they were just joking.

As a brand new golfer with no formal instruction, Alex shot a respectable 110 that day. Thankfully, he acquired the "bug" and two weeks later he went out and bought a set of used clubs. He started taking lessons from the professional at a nearby club.

I can't thank our professional enough because he has helped Alex to solidify his interest in the sport, give up boxing, and play golf every weekend. He watches the golf shows on television. He even reads golf magazines. With professional lessons, he is becoming a very good golfer and he never comes home anymore with black eyes. His new hobby has made a big difference in our lives.

Elena Amado
Boca Raton, Fla.

A Tub of Cold Water Yields Major Dividends

Whatever pearls of wisdom I may have passed along to students about preparing oneself for competition and staying fit, I practiced on myself beginning about two weeks leading up to the 1934 PGA Championship at The Park Club of Buffalo in Williamsville, N.Y.

I had heard that if you wanted to be fit, you had better make a visit to Bill Brown's Health Farm. It was located in Singack, N.Y., on the Hudson River. Bill was renowned in his training methods and I practiced a new diet and exercise regimen.

My wife, Joan, was instrumental in preparing me. Once I had left the health farm, she wouldn't let me slip back into bad habits. I had learned to deal with the heat and my wife would have a light sandwich ready for me after my morning round and get me into a tub of very cold water. There was about four hours between the morning and afternoon matches, and I was drowsy and dozed off for about a half-hour.

Once I awoke, I headed back to the practice tee and prepared for the afternoon round. The weather was more of a factor in 1938 at Shawnee Country Club at Shawnee-on-Delaware, Pa. The humidity was stifling and the other guys were wilting.

But, by the time I got to the course I was feeling like a new man, and it obviously helped my game for those 36-hole matches. In 1934, I defeated my former boss, Craig Wood, in a 38-hole final match. I think I played better over the 173 total holes I needed that year than I did four years later.

In 1938, I finished the week 24-under-par for the 196 total holes I played. I met Sam Snead in the finals at Shawnee Country Club, and won, 8 and 7. Sam was certainly not himself that day. I had a 66 in the morning round and after lunch was 4- or 5-under-par in the afternoon's 29 holes.

Sam was a real gentleman about it and didn't accept any excuses.

"I thought I was the best sand wedge player on Tour," he told reporters, "but Paul hit his 4-wood as close as I hit my wedge. I never took a lesson from Paul. But I guess that match was one. That was enough."

I had won my second PGA Championship title and completed one of my most unforgettable weeks in golf. Many will remember only the margin of victory in 1938. But match play is something very special. Match play golf is a better test of a competitor, and medal (stroke) play is a better test of a golfer.

My staying fit and efforts to just feel good about oneself are two "items" that I've tried to carry in my bag for years.

Paul Runyan
Winner of Two Major Championships
Palm Desert, Calif.

Times Change

At the 1955 Masters, Sam Snead was paired with a young rookie, Jim Cole, in the second round. Snead wasn't having a great tournament and was 4-over-par going into the round. Cole, on the other hand, was striking the ball well and was 4-under-par.

On the 13th hole and the start of the famous Amen corner, a grumpy Snead said to the rookie, "Hey kid, you're really hitting the ball solid. When I was your age I used to turn this par-5 into a par-4 by cutting the corner and hitting my drive over the trees. You're striking the ball so well that this is your chance to make birdie or eagle."

Cole thought for a moment, then teed his ball up just a bit higher, aimed it down the left side over the trees and hit his drive solid and pure. But it wasn't to be. His ball caught the very top of a tree and landed to the left of Ray's Creek, where he proceeded to double bogey the hole.

Shaken up, he bogeyed the 14th and just made par on the 15th. As he settled down on the par-3, 16th hole, he looked at Snead and said, "Mr. Snead, back on the 13th tee I couldn't have hit a drive more perfect than I did. How did you clear those trees?"

Snead coolly looked the young Cole square in the eyes and said, "Kid, when I was your age, those trees were 20 feet shorter!"

Yale Stogel
Hartsdale, N.Y.

Scottish-born Jock Hutchison, the 1920 PGA Champion, also won the 1921 British Open and two Senior PGA Championships, and built a legacy of success and pride for the game.

That Wee Gentleman, Jock, from Scotland

Because I've been in the laugh business just about all of my life, luck would have it that I was invited for many years to a myriad golf functions. To list them as well as the great golf professionals who put up with my wild and errant shots would fill the Smithsonian's new annex.

There was one professional, however, whom I have never forgotten. He was a disarmingly captivating professional of yesteryear who settled in the Fort Lauderdale-Pompano Beach area in his latter years. The old Plantation Country Club in that South Florida City played host to many golfers. Some were top of the heap, others rank and file who just loved the game. Television was in its infancy at this time, but it was a medium that was to give golf, and every facet of the game, the enormous upward thrust, momentum, acceptance and popularity in which it now basks.

Tom Day Sr., manager at the Plantation Club "looked after" one particular gentleman who had been a touring professional back in the 1920 and 1930s.

I used to love playing golf with this elderly gentleman. He was Jock Hutchison, born in St. Andrews, Scotland, and one who indeed grew up with the game.

I'd wander into the golf shop at the club and Tom would say, "Jock's been out on the putting green for an hour."

"But, I'm not late," I countered.

"I know that, but he was out hitting balls on the range for two hours before that."

If there was a love for the game in the history of golf, Jock Hutchison must have been the man who invented it. No, he didn't invent golf; just the passion for it. He was a golf addict, and he taught me to be one.

After slipping into my spikes, I'd wander out the door and Jock would look up, squinting with a sideways glance, "Ah, lad, ready now to go?"

There were no golf cars then. If we picked up another couple of players, local or visitors, I have little memory. But we'd tee off the first tee and begun our trudge down the fairway. Everyone around Plantation knew who Jock was but knew precious little of what he did in golf or for golf.

He was small in stature, slim as a pencil, and he swung the club with the grace of a slow-motion gazelle ... clearing a hurdle. His 5-foot, 7-inch frame always looked exactly the same to me, regardless of which club he swung. Only his putting was different, for he moved his shoulders and arms, as if frozen into a triangular wedge, down the putter shaft to the blade.

There is no way I could begin to guess the times I played golf with Jock. And, when I called him "Mr. Hutchison," he soon put a stop to that.

"Out here on the links, we're all first-namin'," he said.

At first, we would walk the full 18 holes. In his very late years, he slowed and he would stop at the end of nine.

Jock told me many tales of his hey-day in Europe as well as here in our country.

He never discussed his personal woes, but all of us around the club knew he had not had an easy time during his life. He enjoyed, as do most golfers, telling of some of the greats of his day, and how he whipped them. Yet, he was never shy about admitting his losses and close calls when competing.

We'd hike around the course and he was never-ending in trying to correct my countless faults and errors.

I need not include Jock's statistics or achievements. Golf historians provide plenty of that. In this world where heavy emphasis is placed on statistics and celebrity in both golf and other athletic pursuits, it will some day dawn on us that the warmth and humane kindness among the top athletes is what drew us to them.

Jock Hutchison moved into South Florida to be near what little family he had remaining. And, that's where he spent his final years.

Tom Day knew well just who Jock was. And, I was lucky enough to have lived in Plantation, Fla., and to have met and played many golf rounds with him.

Jock was someone who first thought steel shafts were awful, but later warmed to using them. But he stayed with his hickory shafted irons, from the 7-iron through his sand iron and putter. Money-wise, Jock played for nothing more than an ice tea at game's end.

Funny, too, because Jock had his own sense of fairness: The loser of the match had to pay for the drinks.

"Laddie," he would say, "It'll make ya' think and play harder next time!"

Make no mistake about Jock. He was well-known and widely respected throughout the golf world at that time.

Perhaps hard for us to understand, but without television and electronics, the Nicklauses, Palmers, Trevinos, Loves and yes, even the sensational Tiger Woods of today, might be as foreign to some of us as those names of the earliest golf professionals.

There is precious little film of Jock Hutchison. There are brief clips of him and other vintage professionals leading the pack off the first tee at The Masters. He was awarded this honor until shortly before his death.

Then, he would come back to the club at Plantation. And, I'd keep him fortified with ice tea for another year.

Woody Woodbury
Fort Lauderdale, Fla.

Duck Hook

Several years ago, my friend Tom was vacationing by himself, at La Quinta. He became friendly with one of the starters and one evening, the starter called to tell him they needed a fourth the following morning. The next day, Tom arrived at the first tee at 10:00 a.m. and the starter introduced him to a doctor and his wife. He also told him that their fourth would join them at the fifth hole.

Approaching the fifth tee, Tom saw a lone figure sitting in a golf car. The single, obviously friendly, said, "Hello" to the doctor and his wife and then shook hands with Tom. He asked Tom what his handicap was and Tom replied, "An 18." As they were talking, Tom recognized the stranger as Lee Trevino. With a big smile, Lee told Tom, "I will give you two shots on the par-5s and one shot on the par-3s and 4s, but I would like to play for money." My friend Tom gulped and then agreed, and Lee said, "We will play for ten cents."

On the 18th hole, Lee looked at Tom and said, "Well, Tom, we are all even. If I duck hook this shot into the pond, you win." Amazingly, Lee did indeed duck hook the ball then turned to Tom, handed him a dime and said with that famous Trevino smile, "Now you can go back East and tell your pals you beat Lee Trevino in a Nassau."

Vincent Daraio
Rye Brook, N.Y.

And Then There Were Two ...

One of my favorite PGA Professional stories happened awhile ago at the Rio Grande Valley Open in Harlingen, Texas, just after I had received my discharge from the Army Air Corps.

My mentor, George Schneiter, who at that time was the tournament bureau manager, paired me with Jerry Barber and Tommy Bolt. Bolt had the nickname of "Terrible Tommy Bolt" possibly due to his temper on the course, but he certainly was a wonderfully easy-going guy when not competing. The three of us hit good drives on the first hole, leaving short iron shots to the green. Bolt had a three-footer for a birdie, Barber had approximately a six-footer, and I had about a four-footer (all for birdies). Barber holed his putt for a 3, I lipped out my four-footer and, while marking my ball, I inadvertently stepped in Bolt's line.

I was embarrassed and told Mr. Bolt (as I called him) that I was sorry. Mr. Bolt graciously said, "That's OK son, no need to apologize." Mr. Bolt's putt then caught the lip and spun out leaving a six-incher. He became noticeably upset and he then reached out and backhanded it only to lip it out again. Now really upset, he carelessly hit it once more only to have it lip out again. Finally, almost in a rage, he backhanded his ball away from the hole and knocked it clear across the green into the sand trap.

After gaining his composure, Tommy turned to Jerry Barber and asked how many shots he had taken ... he had lost count. Barber replied, "The last time you hit your ball, it was moving, which is a two-stroke penalty, therefore, you lie 8 in the trap."

Mr. Bolt marched into the sand, hit a gorgeous, soft explosion shot that landed one foot from the hole, which he made for a 10 (6-over) on the first hole of the event. I could tell from his eyes that he no longer wanted to play in this event, but he did go on and he clearly re-established himself as a true professional. He birdied the next six holes to get back to even par for the round. At the eighth hole, a par-3 located fairly close to the clubhouse, Mr. Bolt striped a beautiful iron shot that flew just over the flagpole and landed right on the back of the green … a great shot. When we reached the green, Mr. Bolt walked over, picked up his ball, waved "so long" to us and headed for the locker room.

Jerry Barber and I finished the round as a twosome.

Richard Lundahl
PGA Life Member
Sun Lakes, Ariz.

Trophy Winner

Jamie Mulligan has established himself as a special PGA Professional in the Southern California area. Jamie is a patient teacher who always conveys enthusiasm for his students and reminds them what the game is really all about – fun.

But there is another reason why Jamie is special. My wife, an avid golfer, was recovering from breast cancer surgery when she achieved a hole-in-one on a par-3. Although she was very excited, she received almost no recognition at our club. I mentioned this to Jamie who was disappointed that the club wasn't more responsive. A hole-in-one is really a big event for any golfer. A few weeks later Jamie produced a hole-in-one trophy with my wife's name, the date, the hole, and the golf course. This was extremely thoughtful, as he was my coach and only saw my wife occasionally. Clearly, he didn't have to go out of his way to do what he did, but thanks to this professional's integrity, my wife was delighted and that trophy now occupies a special place in our home.

Alan London
Seal Beach, Calif.

Payne and Matt

My family was saddened by the death of Payne Stewart; he was our favorite professional golfer. My son, Matt, who was born with Down Syndrome, began to play golf in the Special Olympics in Texas, when golf became an official event.

Friends of ours gave us tickets to the Shell Houston Open, which is where we met Payne Stewart. As Payne was practicing, Matt recognized him immediately by his attire. I noticed that as Payne lined up a putt, he was looking directly at Matt. Payne suddenly stopped his practice, walked over to Matt, shook his hand, and asked if he could sign Matt's new souvenir golf cap.

Payne chatted with Matt, told him to have a nice day, then strolled off to the number one tee to begin his round. This simple act would probably go unappreciated by most people, but I knew it was something special between him and my son. The memories of that special moment for a young man and his dad were among the things I thought of when I learned of Payne's death. I have now been to other professional golf events and know how unusual Payne's actions were that day especially because it was a competition day. Payne Stewart represents the epitome of what I think a golf professional, on and off the course, is all about. I believe when he entered the gates of Heaven, the Lord said what many of us had said many times ... "Nice shot, Payne."

Clyde McKelvey
Fairfield, Texas

Here's to the Caddies

I never acknowledged the contribution that caddies make to the game of golf until the day I became one, myself. Now, I have the utmost respect for all caddies and quite frankly, don't know how the game of golf existed without them.

My experience as a caddie started back in June 2000. I had a chance to be inside the ropes at The PGA Club Professional Championship held at Oak Tree Country Club in Edmond, Okla. I caddied for Carl Alexander, a club professional from Medford, N.Y. – a class act and a real credit to The PGA.

Carl had a typical tour bag but it seemed to get heavier with each step that I took. In fact, this championship seemed like it was two of the longest 36 holes I had ever walked and I was in pretty good shape at the time.

The first day I caddied I wore long baggy shorts. We were in 96-degree heat. After 18 holes, my inner thighs were badly chaffed, I was sunburned like a lobster, and I was positive that someone had put rocks in the bottom of Carl's bag.

When I woke up the next day, my legs were so sore that I found it difficult to walk, but I knew that I had no choice but to get going and put my pain behind me. I arrived at the course, met Carl, and hoisted the bag over my shoulder. I can still remember thinking, "Just put one foot in front of the other and you'll get through this," as I was off into the blazing heat for another 18 holes. It was tough enough just carrying the bag, not to mention the other duties I was expected to perform – keeping our towel wet, washing balls, cleaning the clubs, retrieving water (for both of us), raking bunkers, and occasionally giving Carl an encouraging pep talk. All this plus the pressure of reading the greens and knowing I had to give him the right line on his putts. Carl Alexander knew it was my first time as a caddie and he knew I was in pain. I think he was helping me as much as I was trying to help him and I'll always respect him for that.

When I watch a tournament now I do something most people never do. I watch *both* the players and the caddies with new found respect.

Larry Dean Snook
Moore, Okla.

Tiger and John Perez

I was playing in a tournament sponsored by Lexus. They were providing a new Lexus 300 sports utility vehicle to anyone who hit a hole-in-one.

I walked out on the 187-yard, par-3 with my 7-wood and smiled at the Lexus witness standing off to the side. My professional told me to think positive … think positive … think positive, so as I approached the ball I mentioned, "Hey, get those keys ready." I am sure the Lexus guy had heard that a dozen times. What he did not know was that I was not kidding. I struck the ball perfectly. It landed on the green and went right into the cup.

Winning a Lexus is not the same as being at the U.S. Open, but for a brief moment this New York chef was at the top of the game. My professional told me, "Now you know how Tiger Woods feels when he wins a major event." I am not sure about that, but I feel real good that John Perez and Tiger Woods are being mentioned in the same story in this book.

John Perez
Brooklyn, N.Y.

Moon Shot

In 1971, Chris Craft, NASA's executive director, and astronaut Alan Shepard, the first American launched into space, asked Jack Harden, head professional at Houston's River Oaks Country Club, to build a special golf club for the Apollo 14 lunar mission.

Jack crafted a unique head out of a 6-iron and Shepard smuggled the club aboard the space ship.

After the moon landing, Shepard announced that he was going to, "Try a little sand shot up here." Because of the bulkiness of his space suit, he had to swing one-handed. In spite of this, he struck the ball perfectly and it sailed an estimated 600 yards in the moon's empty atmosphere.

The ball is still on the moon with Jack Harden's name on it, and his ingenious club is in the USGA Museum at Golf House in Far Hills, N.J.

Pachy Weed
Santa Maria, Calif.

Harold "Jug" McSpaden, who together with Byron Nelson, made up golf's "Gold Dust Twins" of the 1940s.

A Defeat That Even Jug Didn't Mind

Of Jug McSpaden's many accomplishments, he was most proud of whom he had beaten.

"I can honestly say that I beat every great golfer of my time, head to head. Hogan, Snead, Sarazen, Nelson, Hagen, all of them," said McSpaden, who won 26 official and unofficial events before quitting the Tour in 1947.

But nothing delighted him more than a match he didn't win against an unknown golf superintendent in a practice round for a Senior PGA tournament at Kansas City's challenging Loch Lloyd Country Club.

For the whole summer of 1988, McSpaden, who was 80 at the time, worked with Donnie Duren almost every morning on hitting golf balls. Duren, the golf superintendent at Victory Hills Country Club (where McSpaden lived in his home between the 8th and 17th tees), would start each day hitting balls from a hill within eyesight of McSpaden's home.

"He and his wife, Betsy, would be out early having coffee, and he'd yell at me, 'Keep your head down,'" remembers Duren. "He watched me a few days from the porch and then he started coming over and would hold my head down."

"For the whole summer, five days a week, he'd help me. If there was a day I didn't show up, he'd stop past to see why I wasn't there. I had a shag bag with 100 balls and if he wasn't satisfied, we'd go pick them up and I'd hit another 50. Some of the things he taught me felt so awkward but then I'd hit a good shot and it dawned on me he knew what he was talking about. He was a good teacher; he definitely knew what he was talking about."

By the end of that summer, Duren's handicap had dropped from a 19 to a 4 – and established a friendship that took them to various Kansas City courses including Loch Lloyd.

"I must have played with him 40 or 50 times and it was the only time I beat him," says Duren. "I'd started poorly and he said, 'You've got to do this' and had me change something and I started hitting the ball straight. I shot 76; he shot 78 and was happy as a lark. He thought that was the greatest."

"Jug really like helping people, but on his terms. He was hard to get to know but once he got to know you, he'd help you all he could. I think he was leery of people always wanting something."

"We had a young professional who was fascinated with Jug, and who wanted to know how he could get help like I did. I told him just to talk with him, get to know him and not say anything about getting help. But he couldn't wait. He asked Jug one morning if he'd help him and Jug said, 'I get $100 a lesson, how many do you want?'"

McSpaden, who in the mid-1960s had built the world's longest course – 8,101-yard Dub's Dread – was also a guiding force for Duren when Victory Hills (now Painted Hills) was sold and underwent major changes in the layout of the course.

"He and the new owner, Marty Streiff, hit it off and he'd be around just about every day making suggestions," said Duren.

On April 22, 1996, Duren went to the McSpaden house to check on Jug and Betsy, who he hadn't seen for about four days. They were found dead of accidental carbon monoxide poisoning. Jug was 87 years of age.

"Every night Jug would drive his car into the garage and I know he probably had something on his mind and forgot to shut off the motor," said Duren.

"Jug always said he was going to play golf until he was 100 and I think he would have. At 87, he was still shooting in the 70s. I don't think I ever saw him when he didn't shoot his age. He was real excited because that summer he was planning on playing in several Super Seniors events and was really looking forward to playing with the older guys.

"Even today, I still go past the house and look for Jug and Betsy. He was a great golfer – but even a greater friend. I really miss them both."

Alan Hoskins
Sports Columnist
Kansas City Kansan
Kansas City, Kan.

Good Luck Man

I was 85 years old when I received my Half-Century PGA Member Pin in August 1999. At the time it was hard to believe I had been a PGA Professional for 50 years, and had been playing golf for 75 years.

A story I'll always remember occurred on a Sunday morning in 1960, at Airways Golf Course in Fresno, Calif. I was playing in a tournament and was on the fifth hole, which was a par-3. I looked up when it was my turn to shoot and saw Henry Steinhauer on the back of the green about 145 yards away. Henry worked for me in the shop and he had come out to see me for some reason. They had told him where I was, so he had driven his car over and parked just behind the green.

Well, I teed off and watched the ball fly. It bounced on the green and then went right into the hole. Henry immediately ran down to the cup and pulled the ball out and started running towards me. When he arrived, he asked, "Ray, can I have this ball? I've never seen a hole-in-one before!"

I smiled and said, "Yes, Henry, you can have the ball."

About a month later, almost to the day, I was coming up to the ninth, 225 yards away. Again, when it was my turn to shoot, I looked up and there was Henry Steinhauer, standing back of the green on the apron. I fired my shot down the fairway and to my surprise, it also ran right into the cup. Henry immediately ran down, plucked the ball out of the hole and started running towards me. Again he asked me, "Ray, can I have this ball?" He was smiling widely, but this time I shook my head.

"No, Henry, not this time. I'm gonna mount this one myself!"

Well, I think old Henry sparked something in me and I wish he was able to see more of the aces, but he passed away a short time later. I've made 23 holes-in-one all told – the last one on Nov. 12, 1999 – but the two with Henry standing on the back of the green, on the apron, always make me smile in remembrance.

Raymond Forrester
PGA Teaching Professional
Fresno, Calif.

10th Hole Rest Spot

A few years ago, I received a phone call from Linc Oviatt, a very distinguished member at our club. Linc is a lawyer and he was asking permission to spread the ashes of a friend and former president of the Wooster Country Club, Hensley Hobbs, over the 10th fairway in a ceremony in August. Upon his retirement, Hensley had moved to North Carolina where he was fortunate enough to be able to play all the golf he wanted. He had just passed away and one of his final requests was to have his ashes spread over our 10th hole, the site of his only hole-in-one.

The pre-arranged Saturday in August arrived and, that evening at dusk, several family members and friends gathered on our 10th green and bid a fond farewell to Hensley. Through the golf shop windows I began to watch the event, but the phone rang and I was pulled away from the final portion of the ceremony and did not see where they actually put the ashes.

The following morning, I thought of Hensley as my eyes were drawn to the sprinklers that were watering the 10th hole green in front of the golf shop. The morning was uneventful until one of the golfers from the first group of the day returned to the golf shop. He had just played the 10th hole and had come back to complain about a muddy substance that was in the cup on the 10th hole and was now on his ball, glove, and putter.

Remembering the ceremony the night before and the morning sprinklers, I responded with the truth; "That's Hensley." I do not think the member really knew the significance of my comment but, thankfully, he quietly left the shop.

Gary L. Welshhans
PGA Professional
Wooster (Ohio) Country Club

It's All Luck!

I had been playing golf for over 50 years before finally making my first hole-in-one at The Landings on Skidaway Island in Savannah, Ga. Being quite excited, I couldn't wait to tell my good friend, Tommy Hilliard, then Director of Golf at The Landings. His reaction was, "Aw! It's all luck!"

Tommy had never made a hole-in-one, which surprised me, as he was an excellent golfer. As luck (or skill) would have it, during the next 15 months, I had two more aces and, as it was my nature, I needled Tommy as to why he hadn't yet achieved that feat.

To get even with me after my third ace, he put in our weekly magazine, "Congratulations to Bill Lutz on making his third hole-in-one in 15 months. Bill said, 'There's nothing to it, I fully expect to get another before the year is out.'"

You can imagine the ribbing I took from the guys at the club when that was published! Tommy had really gotten even for the abuse I had been giving him. But amazingly, only two weeks later I scored my fourth ace! All Tommy could do is shake his head in total disbelief.

Reality soon set in and my streak ended. But I am happy to report that Tommy, now director of golf at The Ocean Reef Club in Key Largo, Fla., has finally got a hole-in-one under his belt. Let's see if he can now make three more before the year's over!

William Lutz
Stuart, Fla.

We Wear Many Hats

I am sure that every golf professional has had many wonderful and memorable days throughout their careers and I would like to share a particular favorite of mine.

In 1999, I was playing in a pro-member tournament at Bear's Paw Country Club in Naples, Fla. I knew that I was going to be a bit late, due to a prior commitment, so I informed my fellow golf professional ahead of time. However, I did promise to be at the club in time to tee-off with my three companions.

About 10 minutes prior to the start of the shotgun format, I was heading to the clubhouse to locate my group and I spotted our ranger running toward me. He informed me that my fellow golfers were waiting for me on the 17th hole. When I arrived, I found Mrs. Smith, a spry woman, about 4-foot-8, in her mid-70s, looking distraught. She was pointing to her left leg and exclaiming, "We decided to hit a few balls on the range while we were waiting and I got hit by a golf ball!" After inspecting it, I told her that she should consider dropping out of the tournament since her leg was swollen and bruised. She quickly said, "No, I have been looking forward to this for three weeks! I will continue." So, off we went and everything went smoothly … until we reached the par-3 eighth hole.

I was just starting to relax and enjoy the game when, all of a sudden, Mrs. Jones threw her golf club in the air and began running and screaming. She screamed to her husband, "Honey, I was stung by a bee!" I was thinking, "How bad could it be?" Well, it was pretty bad since she was severely allergic to bees. Mr. Jones quickly ran to the cart and retrieved a tattered looking first aid kit that appeared to be every bit of five years old. He produced a needle filled with medicine.

Her neck was swelling so fast that I began to panic. I grabbed my cell phone to call 911, when suddenly she yelled, "Don't you dare call an ambulance! I will be OK after my injection!" Mr. Jones drew back the needle and stuck it into his wife's leg. She screamed, "It didn't go off!" He drew his arm back again and slammed it harder than before. "It still didn't go off," Mrs. Jones loudly moaned. "Did you remove the safety cap?" Mr. Jones was noticeably shaken and, with a dumbfounded look on his face, he proceeded to remove the safety cap and stuck it into her leg a third time. Unfortunately, the needle was backwards and he stuck it into his own thumb. He let out a yell like I have never heard before. By this time, the group playing behind us appeared. Luckily, they had medication in their cart and offered Mrs. Jones a dose. Now, I was begging Mrs. Jones to let me call an ambulance, but she emphatically yelled, "No!"

In a little while, Mrs. Jones started feeling better so she talked me into proceeding with the game. However, that did not stop me from punching "9-1-1" and preparing to hit the "send" button, if necessary. After several more holes, things had again calmed down and I thought I might as well enjoy myself and relax as both Mrs. Smith and Mrs. Jones now appeared to be fine. However, just about when I thought the day would turn out fine, Mr. Jones looked at me and said, "I don't know if I can continue. Look at my hand." His thumb and part of his palm had turned *green*. Apparently, he had a reaction to his wife's medication. My stomach was now turning flips. I got my cell phone out and told them that we had to return to the clubhouse immediately to meet the ambulance. Mrs. Jones ordered, "Put that phone away! We will not be going in until the game is finished. My husband will be fine." I could not believe my ears. Mr. Jones looked at me, shrugged and said, "OK."

We finished the round and, believe it or not, placed second in the tournament. As a courtesy, and out of curiosity, I called the next day to inquire about all three of my companions. Mrs. Smith was relaxing at home, Mrs. Jones was playing in the Ladies Day Tournament, and Mr. Jones spent the night in the local emergency room. I am happy to report that he was also fine.

Some people interpret the life of a PGA Professional as exciting and glamorous and sometimes, it really is. Needless to say, our motto as PGA Professionals is very true; "We wear many hats."

Doug Burnham
Head Professional
The Club at Grandézza
Estero, Fla.

The Journey of the Black Widow

If you are very lucky you might experience a moment in time when the direction your life should take suddenly makes sense. A defining moment, if you will, when your destiny, your purpose, is laid out before you, like a golden road waiting to be followed. Nothing seems clearer at that instant and even if it fades almost as suddenly as it appears, the memory can carry you through a lifetime.

When he was young, my father, Dennis Garman, bought a golf club that the professional who sold it declared that no one could hit. Dad had a natural talent on the golf course, so he bought the club at a bargain price with confidence that he could, indeed, hit it. It was a Black Widow driver, one of the first of the big-headed clubs, and a beauty to look at. While Dad's skill on the golf course was what might be labeled as natural and fluid, he worked hard to improve his game. He appeared to play with an ease and grace envied by those who watched. At an early age, he believed his future was going to be somewhere on the golf course. Visions of PGA Championships kept him going through a tumultuous childhood and beyond, into his teenage years. The Black Widow was fun for him to play, giving him power to lengthen his drives and enabling him to hit it where others could not.

Unfortunately, the Vietnam War was raging back then and Dad, like so many of his peers, enlisted in the service. However, fate took the opportunity that she often does to throw a curve into his life. Holding a phosphorus bomb that was on the base as a teaching tool, Dad squatted down to examine it closer and the hands that were magic on a golf club, slipped. The bomb was live, not plaster-filled as it should have been, and it exploded into a wall of flames.

At first, his parents were told that Dad, then 20, was badly burned and was not expected to live. Then they were informed that he would never walk, never have children, and live a short and painful life. After an agonizing year in the hospital, he did indeed walk out ... but into a life very different than the one he had imagined. He tried playing again but his right hand had been so badly damaged in the explosion that he was forced to wear a protective cast. His feet bled after short walks in shoes that would never be comfortable again. The skin on his right hand was so damaged that it split at the slightest bump despite the cast, and the skin on his left hand would crack and bleed in anything but perfect weather. The sulfur from the bomb had worked down into his bones causing painful ulcers and countless surgeries. Golf was put aside as a younger man's unfulfilled dream.

In a love story written at another time, Dad married my mother, Becky, and soon my sister and I were born, proving the doctors wrong once more. He fell into a life of business and I believe he was content. The Black Widow was given away shortly after the accident and was passed around from golfer to golfer, never really being played the way that a young man had once played it, in magical strong hands.

Nearly 20 years after that moment in boot camp, the beautiful black club with the red stripe down the middle inexplicably found its way to my father once more. An uncle suggested he try it out, unknowingly giving him back the club that Dad had once admired and had so easily played on the golf courses of Northern California so many years ago. It rested awkwardly next to the fireplace of our new golf-front home that we had recently moved into. My father had always wanted to live on a golf course, maybe to awaken the dreams that had lain in a troubled sleep, maybe just to enjoy the breathtaking view of the canyon. Either way, as a young girl I admired the smooth head of the club, the shiny blackness of it, the way it felt so top heavy in my inexperienced hands. I remember innocently asking my father about why it sat there unused, why it was never played. And in the way that is magic only between fathers and daughters, my father told me the story of how he came to twice own the Black Widow. In demonstration, without thought of his cast that lay forgotten on the counter, he took me out to the back deck where the fourth hole, par-5 lay below and swung the club with the ease of a natural golfer. In the instant that the club left the earth and made its way, unwavering, into the air, Dad's expression changed. He had instantly become that young man with a dream to be a professional golfer again. The swing came with ease, whipped through the air with the whistle that is music to a golfer's ears, and the impact with the golf ball startled me. My father, so familiar to me, became someone I had never seen before. He was suddenly a man with dreams – someone with the desire to fulfill those dreams once more. In that instant, he defined who he was, not just to me, but to himself.

The ball that Dad hit that day seemed like a perfect shot and in my mind is still flying somewhere over the California hills. What happened next, however, is truly amazing. For four years following that moment my father worked on rebuilding his golf game, toughening his hands, which seemed to bleed all the time, because he played without his cast. Soon our family left the state and moved to North Carolina, where golf courses abound. After immense hard work and countless disappointments, Dennis Garman is now the PGA Professional at the beautiful Beech Mountain Golf Course. I don't know what has happened to the Black Widow driver, but I don't think that it really matters. It served the purpose that it was intended to serve. It was more than a club, it was the stuff that dreams are made of.

Kiki Garman
Mooresville, N.C.

Steven Cope, at age 9, receives instruction from his "buddy," PGA Professional Chris Anderson of Wilmington, Del.

A Buddy for Life

Most people believe professional golfers just help people with their golf game, but that's not true. Many go far beyond and help people with their lives.

Awhile ago, I remarried and one of my husband's children, Steven, was 3 years old when I became his stepmother. He was born with spina bifida, which can cause nerves controlling the legs, skin and internal organs to be damaged resulting in paralysis, a lack of sensation, and bowel and bladder dysfunction. Additionally, spina bifida almost always is accompanied by a condition known as hydrocephalus – where fluid builds up in the brain.

Steven has undergone 30 operations in his life starting when he was only two days old. He wears braces now, which run the full length of his legs and include his feet, because he has no control of his feet or ankles. He walks with the aid of arm crutches, but can only walk very short distances. Because he does not have bladder function, Steven also must catheterize himself every three hours, which he has been doing since he was 6 years old and must do a bowel program every other evening.

In 1993, Steven was one of five poster children selected by the Variety Club of Philadelphia to work with five PGA Professionals from the Philadelphia PGA Section in its Buddy Program.

Steven met Chris Anderson, an assistant professional at Fieldstone Golf Club in Wilmington, Del. They became instant friends. Chris would teach Steven golf's fundamentals and have him hitting the ball off a high tee from a wheelchair. It was difficult at first, but with practice all the kids in the program did very well.

After the initial meeting, Chris began to see more of Steven and take him to Philadelphia Phillies baseball games and movies. Steven's health condition worsened and he needed additional specialized care. Chris had an uncle who was on the board of directors of the Alfred I. Dupont Hospital for Children. Chris arranged for a doctor specializing in spina bifida to see Steven. Thanks to Chris, we have been under the care of the Alfred I. Dupont Hospital ever since.

In 1999, when Steven turned 16, his spinal column had deteriorated to the point that he needed to undergo additional and very risky surgery to fuse vertebra. Doctors also inserted a rod through his spinal column.

Chris was there every step of the way. He called Steven several times before the surgery to wish him well and later he joined me in the waiting room of the hospital. After four hours, Chris went and got us food. By the time Steven was brought into the recovery room, he was so pale and with no color. I was very worried.

Chris said something to me, and when Steven heard Chris' voice, he didn't open his eyes but raised his right arm and gave us both the "thumbs up" sign.

As Steven recovered, Chris was a constant visitor. He even stayed overnight in the hospital room with Steven, one night, sleeping on a cot. Also, they had what Steven called a "Guys' Night In" with pizza while they watched movies. Chris had given to Steven a shag bag that he had been given by his father. Steven continued to go to the golf lessons and Buddy Program functions. Chris still comes to see Steven on holidays and calls regularly.

Steven has improved in so many ways, though he is still bound to a wheelchair. His grades are good and his self-esteem is high. Steven said, "Chris means a lot to me. He's always there for me."

Chris Anderson has become a member of our family and has given us so much. I realize that many PGA Professionals give back to their community, but Chris has gone way over and above the duties of a golf professional and friend.

Without the Variety Club's Buddy Program, Steven wouldn't have a social life ... without Chris, Steven would have a very difficult life. Our family is blessed to know him.

Bette L. Cope
Reading, Pa.

Brother, Can You Spare a Dime?

Although the fashionable swing doctors and sports psychologists have tried very hard to exploit and develop every minute detail of the game of golf, old-fashioned gamesmanship remains, undoubtedly, one of the immeasurable quantities of competition.

There are also times, of course, when a golfer with "rabbit ears" can be distracted from his game by innocent sounds or, as the wry writer P.G. Wodehouse once inferred, "The uproar of the butterflies in the adjoining meadows."

PGA Professional Ken Allard, who was head professional at Radrick Farms Golf Club in Ann Arbor, Mich., at the time, was working his way over Southern Hills Golf Club in the opening round of the 1977 United States Open Championship. Allard was definitely "on his game" this day and was only slightly aware of the dedicated golf mavens behind the ropes who swarmed and scrambled from each tee shot to gain a close-up view of his performance.

By the third hole, Allard began to be bothered by some distraction, although he wasn't certain precisely why.

By the fourth tee, he caught himself anticipating the invading stimulus, and by the fifth, was devoting precious swing thoughts to discerning what the noise was that he was hearing.

The noise was ever so slight … it was slightly familiar … it had no particular cadence or rhythm, but it seemed to intensify each time the head of his oversized driver nestled at address behind his teed ball, or as he was about to stroke a critical putt.

It was on the sixth green, when Allard marked his ball with a dull dime, that he realized that the sound he was hearing was coins jingling in the pocket of a spectator. He was pleased with himself at solving the mystery and chagrined that he hadn't recognized the tinny audio earlier, but he had business to do on the green – lining-up a snaking 30-footer – so he cleared his head, tended to the business at hand, and safely two-putted the hole.

As he walked to the seventh tee, Allard had a dual purpose in mind. He needed to play proficiently, but to do so, he needed to eliminate his distraction by first locating the source of the collision of coins.

Clearly, the task was not easy and his "coin" thoughts were now stronger than his "golf" thoughts. At the seventh tee, Allard went through the motions of his pre-shot ritual without a single thought of golf. His ears were stretching like deep space listening devices, and his senses were scanning like sonar, with his eyes darting and sending out "pings" – as might a submariner searching the sea.

Allard sensed the gallery growing impatient, or at least growing puzzled, as was his own caddie, by the sight of him frozen at address position without so much as a waggle. The pressure was mounting. Allard's bundled nerves gave way as might a bowstring held too long, and his shortened takeaway coupled with his hurried down stroke and tentative follow-though combined to produce one of the ugliest serpentines ever struck by a professional golfer.

The sound that came from his lips was one of both torment and resignation, but it was quickly cut off lest he give the hometown crowd the slightest indication of concern. With a deep breath, Allard confidently marched down the fairway to forage for his ball.

On his way he strolled along with the gallery and suddenly stopped dead in his tracks as an older fellow passed in front of him … jingle … clang … jingle … clang …

Allard had spotted the coin-laden calamity that was impacting his game as he toyed with the contents of his pockets at his moment of tension.

Allard's caddie located his ball and it was with a sense of relief that he played the rest of the hole, making bogey. Allard took comfort in knowing that the mystery was solved and that soon his nemesis would be dispensed of.

Allard adjusted his visor and made a beeline from the seventh green toward the eighth tee, but anyone watching would not have seen the deceleration in his step the very minute he realized he was walking into a paradoxical predicament. If he charged the gallery and accused the man of jingling and jangling his coins on purpose, he might rile the crowd against him. If the older spectator was inadvertently moving his money to relieve tension, he could embarrass the gent. It was a delicate matter, to be sure.

Step by step, yard by yard, Allard walked and figured, walked and figured.

Once again, the crowd waited for him as he dawdled. His opponent, club drawn with honors, waited for him to climb to the tee, where Allard's caddie had already drawn and unsheathed his driver.

Allard reached the tee, purposefully scanned the crowd, and fumbled slightly with his club, somewhat to the annoyance of his fellow competitor, who was eager to settle into his tee shot.

Suddenly, the color flushed back into Allard's face as he reached a solution. With new confidence, the bounce returned to his step as he casually walked over to the oblivious, yet noisy, observer.

The face of Allard's opponent bore a look of "now what?" as he stood between the tee markers watching Allard approach the gallery.

Allard pulled a bill from his pocket, and, without making eye contact, whispered innocently out the side of his mouth.

"Hey, pal, got change for a dollar?"

Michael Patrick Shiels
Wyandotte, Mich.

An Old Photograph

In 1943, when I was a young boy living in Quincy, Ill., I wrote a letter to Sam Snead and asked him for an autographed picture. He was stationed at the Naval Air Station in San Diego at the time.

He sent me a small picture and a letter that encouraged me to keep "my nose to the grindstone" and keep working on my golf game. Later, I had the letter and his picture put in an expensive frame and placed on my wall.

I followed Mr. Snead's advice and encouragement and worked very hard on my game. In fact, over the years I played in many amateur tournaments and in 1969, I became a PGA member.

In 1997, while visiting in Myrtle Beach, S.C., I stopped in Mr. Snead's restaurant and asked the manager to give the framed letter to Sam the next time he came in. I wrote him a note along with the picture and thanked him for his support when I was only 14. The manager said he didn't know whether Sam wanted to keep the picture or not.

About two months later, I was giving a golf lesson at a club in St. Louis. My student had just told me that while playing in a tournament at Bay Hill, Arnold Palmer had walked up to him and asked if it was OK if he played a few holes with him. My student said that he was speechless.

About half an hour later, the assistant professional came out to the practice tee and said that my wife had just received a call from Sam Snead and he wanted me to call him as soon as possible. You should have seen the look on my student's face!

When I called, he said that he was very happy that I had returned his letter and photo after 54 years and that he would mount it on his wall. He later sent a letter to me with the following comment:

"Received the picture and letter of 1943. Thanks a million. I was pleased you became a professional and are now looking back at what you accomplished in golf."

Roger A. Williams
PGA Life Member
Lake St. Louis, Mo.

I Almost Missed It

On Monday, May 11, 1998, I called Mr. Stacey Jourdon, with the Northern Texas PGA Section, concerning my two days of volunteer work at the Byron Nelson Golf Classic in Irving, Texas. My service work would include working with juniors at our NTPGA swing booth on Thursday afternoon and returning on May 16, to assist with the media and scoring. Stacey explained the where, what, and how of getting into the tournament. However, my enthusiasm was shattered by the three worst words ever spoken to most golf professionals, "By the way, Sam, on Saturday you will need to wear a *coat and tie.*" I could not believe my ears! Coat and tie? The forecast was for temperatures in the mid-90s. But I needed the PDP points and Stacey was not going to change his mind.

For the next five days, including the drive from Fort Worth to Irving, I was *not* a happy camper. Have you ever seen a zebra mixed in with a herd of thoroughbreds? That was all I could visualize. I finally decided to wear a pair of navy blue slacks, white shirt, navy PGA logoed tie and my camel colored sport coat with the Northern Texas PGA pocket crest.

As I boarded the bus on Saturday for the main gate, the looks of disbelief began. Upon entry I stopped and purchased a Lord Byron style straw hat to protect my old bald head and off to the central scoring trailer I headed. Within moments I walked by three young men who said in passing, "Wow! Did you see that guy? He is a PGA official." My first thought as I continued on my way was "cool." They had noticed my pocket crest. I could not remember the last time I had worn the crest, but this seemed like the right time and place.

This happened several more times before I could reach the scoring trailer. I was met at the front door by Mr. Bill Schilling, who welcomed me and said, "Man, but don't you look nice. We will send you to the 18th green to the ladies scoring tent."

As I started back toward 18, I ran into a friend who also works with my wife, Linda. He said, "Man, you really look great … and so official!" About that time a small girl approached me and asked if I was a tournament official. I told her, "No" but I was representing the Northern Texas PGA.

Arriving at the scoring tent, positioned just to the right of the 18th green, I was greeted by six or seven ladies who all made comments about how grateful they were to have official representation from the PGA and how nice I looked. My head was getting so big; I almost had to exchange my Lord Byron hat for a larger size.

I was offered food and drink and told to make myself at home. Stacey dropped by to say hello and moments after he left the tent, a representative of the PGA Tour came up and introduced himself. He explained that I was in charge of verification and collection of scores turned in at the completion of play. He left me with a few more instructions and then the reality of my job and purpose really started to sink in.

While I was watching a group of player's approach the 18th green, I sensed a commotion at the other end of the tent. As I turned to check out the noise, I suddenly came face to face with Byron Nelson and his lovely wife, Peggy. After catching my breath and introducing myself, the coat and tie issue was immediately resolved. Mr. Nelson said, "Sam, you sure look nice. I hope you don't get too warm." I then explained that anything less than a coat and tie would not be worthy of the setting. Mr. and Mrs. Nelson took their positions in two beautiful wing back chairs placed to overlook the 18th green. As players walked off the green and into the scoring tent, they were greeted by the Nelsons.

During the next few hours I was privileged to be one-on-one with some of the world's greatest players. Names like Mickleson, Watson, Sutton, Couples, Furyk, O'Meara, Tway, Leonard, Pavin, Tiger Woods, and the list just kept going! When I didn't have three world class players in front of me, I was standing right behind the chair of one of the greatest players to ever play our game; Lord Byron Nelson.

It was really tough duty, especially since there was a wonderful Texas breeze blowing through the tent. It crossed my mind several times that my position was priceless. No ticket could be bought for this spot. What was required was a membership card in The PGA of America.

I have had my card for almost 23 years now and I have never been so proud to be a part of such a wonderful association of men and women. That afternoon of volunteer service work was equal to, and maybe better than, my walk onto the first tee at St. Andrews, Scotland in 1983.

With sleeves rolled up, tie and coat in hand, I stepped into the bus for my return ride back to the parking lot. I sat quietly, listening to the exhausted golf patrons discuss the golf shots they had seen the players hit, the clubs used and what they were wearing. My eyes slowly filled up as I thought about how beautiful my afternoon was. The shots I had seen and then to have those players sitting across the table from me. Mr. and Mrs. Nelson only inches away from me all afternoon, and I had to think ... I almost missed it because I didn't want to wear a tie!

Sam Knight
PGA Life Member
Fort Worth, Texas

What Goes Around Comes Around

In 1955, The Lewiston High School golf team of Lewiston, Idaho, was favored to win the Idaho State High School Championship. The only thing standing in their way was a 400-plus mile drive to the southern portion of Twin Falls, and a golf course they had never seen. The task didn't seem so insurmountable in the eyes of my brother, John, his four teammates, or their coach. In fact, they received permission from the school administration to begin their journey a few days early so they could play the golf course a couple of times before the tournament. Everything seemed to be going as planned. The daylong car ride was uneventful. The two days of practice on the golf course went well. Even the weather was cooperating – warmer and sunnier than usual for the middle of May. The night before the event, the team was confident that it could bring home the school's first-ever state golf championship.

Excited, the boys woke early the next morning in anticipation of winning the title. As they hurriedly dressed, one looked out the curtained window to see if it would be warm enough not to need a sweater. To his surprise he was looking at about four inches of fresh snow on the ground!

As the tournament officials huddled, it became evident that they needed to secure a golf course at a lower elevation to play the championship. The Buhl Country Club on the Snake River was selected. All the teams traveled the 30 miles to Buhl, filled with uncertainty about playing on an unknown course. Unfortunately, Lewiston lost the Championship by one stroke to Twin Falls.

Flash forward to 16 years later – the Lewiston High School golf team was having a great season. We were, without a doubt, the best golf team in Northern Idaho. As the year progressed, the thought of bringing home the first-ever state golf championship was, once again, on all of our minds. The tournament was to be held in the southern portion of the state – in Twin Falls – on a golf course only I had played. My brother was practicing law in Twin Falls and when I visited him, we would play the course.

As the tournament neared, we planned our strategy. We received special permission from the school administrators to leave a few days early so we could practice on the golf course. The 400-plus mile trip was uneventful. We had a few days of good practice getting to know the golf course. It was unusually warm for mid-May, and we were all wearing shorts. The night before the tournament we were confident that victory was within our grasp. At long last, a state golf championship!

You guessed it. We awakened the next morning to four inches of fresh snow! And the officials sent us to Buhl Country Club to play the tournament. But this tale took a different turn this time around. Lewiston High School won its first state golf championship, defeating Twin Falls by *one* stroke! And my brother, who explained the irony to me, saw it all.

Bill Rosholt
PGA Professional
La Grande (Ore.) Country Club

A Touch of Class

I was fortunate enough to attend the 1999 Williams World Championship in Arizona. At the end of the tournament, Phil Mickelson was signing autographs as he walked to the clubhouse. Just then, a young boy – maybe 9 years old – ran up to him and said, "Sir, do you know where Tiger is?" The little boy showed no recognition of Phil Mickelson whatsoever.

Phil, being the exceptional professional that he is, turned to him gently and with a wide smile, answered the boy, "I'll bet he's on the practice tee, son … right over there," and he pointed the way. The real professionals don't let their fame go to their heads. They stay regular guys and Mickelson is a professional with tremendous class and confidence.

John L. Curzon
Englewood, Colo.

A focused Raymond Floyd on his way to winning the 64th PGA Championship in 1982 at Southern Hills Country Club in Tulsa, Okla.

It's About the Shoes

The year was 1965. It was my first Masters. I shot 68 the first day and was three shots behind the leader, Gary Player.

For the second round, I checked my pairing and discovered that I would be playing with Arnold Palmer. On Friday, I arrived at the golf course two hours before my starting time to avoid any possible traffic – and to be totally relaxed and prepared for the round.

When I got to my locker, there were dozens of telegrams and messages from my friends and writers stopping me for interviews. I got so caught up in the moment that when I arrived at the practice tee, I looked down to discover that I was still wearing my street shoes.

I sheepishly rushed back to the locker room, changed my shoes, and proceeded to shoot 81 and miss the cut!

Jack Nicklaus shot 271 that year to break Ben Hogan's record by three shots. In 1976, I also shot 271 to tie Jack's record and win my first Masters!

Raymond Floyd
Winner of Four Major Championships
1989 U.S. Ryder Cup Captain
Palm Beach, Fla.

A Candlelight Dinner, with Buzzsaws
in Two-Part Harmony

When Hurricane Gloria visited the Northeast on Friday, Sept. 27, 1985, she also spawned a series of small tornadoes. One of these storms cut a diagonal swathe through Thorny Lea Golf Club in Brockton, Mass. My wife, Barbara, and I were at Thorny Lea as part of the corporate golf team for Foot-Joy who served as the title sponsor of the ninth Foot-Joy PGA Assistant Professional Championship.

This storm had its own set of "local rules." It struck the course near the 17th tee, then cut through to the 16th green and veered across to the sixth fairway, before exiting near the back of the fourth green. According to the longtime residents, this was one of the worse storms ever in the area. Some 300 trees – most two-feet in diameter – were lost on this gem of a course. It would have been easy to cancel the championship, scheduled only five days later on Oct. 2-4, but the club and Foot-Joy Chairman Dick Tarlow agreed that somehow, the show would go on.

What transpired after Gloria's retreat became the greatest example of teamwork I've witnessed between a PGA Professional's staff, club members, and a community.

Thorny Lea's head professional at the time, John Oteri, together with superintendent Joe Rybka and club golf chairman Lou Saba, deserved medals of honor. They spearheaded volunteers, including Brockton area schoolchildren who were allowed out of school the following Monday. Representatives of nearby clubs joined them in an attempt to clear the course of the massive debris.

In 1985, it also was a time of limited technology; there were no cell phones to aid our communication, there was no Internet to e-mail to the rest of the world, and we were without electricity for several days. Our food at the club was prepared on a gas grill. Despite the inconveniences, our Tuesday pro-am went off without a hitch. Even our pro-am dinner on Tuesday night had a surreal atmosphere – still without electricity, guests were served by candlelight.

During the day, you heard the constant drone of buzzsaws cutting through an amazing amount of fallen timber. The volunteers raked and moved the limbs to the edge of the second cut of rough. By the time the first group of the Tuesday pro-am stepped to the first tee, all debris had been removed through the 13th green. The crews rushed to get the remaining holes cleared after that.

The tournament went on without delay, and the 41 assistant professionals from The PGA's Sections, along with four international players, were amazed that they were competing on schedule on a course that just days before, had been a disaster. This was a championship event where the team behind the ropes delivered as much as the teams on the course!

Our company always believed in delivering a quality product, and the golf club loved the tournament and the players. They refused to see it cancelled. They believed in themselves and the good of those people who lived in the community.

This is the spirit of golf. It is a game that enriches us, tests our character, and forms a bond among players worldwide. The PGA Professionals I've worked with over the years share a common bond of helping others. The 1985 championship in Brockton, Mass., will remain as special to me as any major championship. It *was* a major in more ways than I ever would have imagined.

Jim Ireland
Past Vice President
Titleist/FootJoy Worldwide
Palm Beach Gardens, Fla.

Club Call

In 1990, I was playing at the Royal Hong Kong Golf Club in the Hong Kong Open Pro-Am with the British Professional Roger Chapman. As we came to the 18th hole after a most enjoyable round, Roger, who had never played the course, turned and with a quizzical look on his face asked me, "Rob, what club do you normally take on this hole?"

I replied, "A driver, 5-iron, a couple of wedges, and two or three putts … but for you? A driver, 9-iron and one putt should be plenty!"

Where upon we all burst out laughing. Long live pro-ams.

Robert Henderson
City Golf Club
Kowloon, Hong Kong

Class Jitters for a New Professional

During my first year as head professional at the Burlington Golf Club in Iowa, I was trying to do all the right things to begin my career. One project included scheduling and conducting clinics for beginning women players.

The registration was proceeding very well that first spring on the job, and some of the husbands were anxious to see what the new professional could do while teaching their wives a very challenging game. Being very conscientious, I was working extra hard to ensure that I covered everything from "A to Z" in my clinic. I wanted to impress those husbands. I scheduled one clinic per week over a five-week period. Then, three weeks into the program, a couple of husbands decided to take their wives out late in the evening for a few holes to see what they had learned. I was pretty confident the ladies would perform quite well. So, out they went in a small caravan of golf cars. They returned fairly early, I thought.

I saw one of the husbands smirk and he got out of his golf car and approached me.

"I thought you were teaching the ladies everything about the game?"

Half in shock, I thought, "Oh no, what did I forget?"

One of the other husbands then informed me that on the first hole, as they were preparing to putt on the front portion of the green, one of the wives was stalking the back of the green like she was searching for a missing contact lens. Finally, one of the husbands called out, "Excuse me, but what are you looking for?" She said, "Why, the other holes!"

As it turned out, I had not thought to tell my students that all the greens on the course don't have six cups like the lush putting green in front of the clubhouse.

The "cups rule" has been a part of my beginner's curriculum ever since.

Jock Olson
PGA Master Professional
Interlachen Country Club
Edina, Minn.

Lost Wager

I have been involved in various capacities within the golf industry most of my life; and, my son is currently a Class A PGA Professional.

Back in the mid 1960s, I attended the Greater Greensboro Open at the Starmount Forest Golf and Country Club.

We had a lounge area behind the locker room and I was chatting with 10 or 12 of the tour players, including Frank Beard, Joe Campbell and Sam Carmichael.

As we were talking, Dave Hill walked into the room following his practice round. Dave was a fine golfer. He achieved 13 victories during his career. An amazing feat considering he was also the most fined player in PGA Tour history. I found it impossible not to love Dave Hill. He was among the most loyal and honest men I have ever met in the golf game. He was also one of the most fearless. If he didn't like you, he'd look you in the eye and tell you so. If you spoke an untruth, he'd call you a liar right to your face.

Well, Dave announced to all the tour players assembled in the lounge, "Ken Still is playing so good that no one is going to beat him this week." Ken was a journeyman player whose long career only included one win.

Dave's announcement was met with varying degrees of incredulity, including various challenges. This prompted Dave to say, "I've got $500 that says he'll beat everyone in this room."

Joe Campbell, nicknamed "the Golden Boy," whose résumé included four tour victories, an NCAA Championship, and Rookie of the

Year honors, looked around the room and said, "I'll take that bet!" In the mid 1960s, a $500 bet was a significant amount of money.

History recorded that Sam Snead won that tournament. However, history makes no mention of the fact that of all those present in the locker room at the time of Dave's wager, the only person to beat Ken Still that week was Dave Hill himself.

What an ironic way to lose your own bet!

John K. Garrity
Bridgeport, Conn.

The Forgotten Award

The summers of 1965 and 1966 held some of the best memories of my life. When you're eight years old and golf is your life, how could it get any better? My daily routine was to be on my red bike by 6:30 a.m., heading toward the Frankfort Country Club in Frankfort, Ind. I would usually beat the club professional, Mr. Raidy, to the golf shop. I worked in the bag room and I can still smell the combination of grass and pine to this day. I remember when we had pine racks built for club storage. The good news was that it enabled us to store twice the amount of clubs ... the bad news, it caused twice the amount of work for me, cleaning the clubs!

Each morning, I would place set after set into the bucket to soak and then I would wipe them down. And each morning, I would watch as the same members would come in and tell Mr. Raidy the same old golf stories they had told the previous day. I look back in amazement at how he would seem so interested in their every word ... after those years, I told myself that I would never bore people with stories about my golf game. Now, at age 43, I actually think that people are *interested* in hearing about every one of my shots! (It must be a sickness that golfers develop).

After I finished cleaning all the sets, it was time for Mr. Raidy to let the assistant professional take over, and he would have me follow him over to the 10th hole, which was right next to the swimming pool. He would proceed to hit 100-200 shag balls, having me stand about 130 yards out, and pick up each one. More than once, I got "beaned" on the top of the head with a ball because I was busy watching the girls at the pool instead of paying attention to the incoming artillery.

That summer was also very special to me for other reasons. Not only did I receive some of the greatest golf lessons that I have been able to carry over into adulthood and ultimately pass along to my three children, but it was the summer I received my award.

Mr. Raidy hosted the club dinner and with my mom and dad in the audience, along with all the club members and all the great golfers, John Raidy called *my name*! Lots of things went through my mind as I walked up to the front of the room. When Mr. Raidy reached over to hand me the silver cup with my name engraved on it, I had tears in my eyes. As I look back, I can remember Mr. Raidy taking the time to give me weekly lessons, the patience he had, and how he instilled in me the importance of golf etiquette, following the rules, and treating the members and the course with respect. But to this day, I still don't know what the award was for. I think he made up something just because he knew how much working at his club meant to me. He was a very special golf professional.

Mark Wainscott
Carmel, Ind.

The King, a Camera and a Rare Bird

I was playing in my fourth career PGA Championship in August 1993 at Inverness Club in Toledo, Ohio, and it was destined to be a memorable week.

Fellow PGA Professional Ron McDougal and I were just about to tee off on the first hole of a practice round when someone emerged from the crowd. He asked if we had room for one more in our game. It was Arnold Palmer.

As it turned out, Arnold and my father-in-law each attended Wake Forest University and had played on the golf team at the same time.

At one point in the round after making several pretty lengthy putts, Arnold turned to me and said, "Son, don't ever lose that putting stroke." I was very touched to say the least.

Before the first round, my wife, Margie, armed with our video camera, picked up a new assignment while joining the gallery. The PGA of America had asked her to provide amateur footage for a film they were producing of club professionals who earn a berth in the PGA Championship.

But after about nine holes, I became worried that the camera's rechargeable battery was running down. So, I told Margie to stop filming every shot.

We reached the 13th hole, a 515-yard, par-5 that seemed to fit my game. I hit what I felt was a perfect drive and had 222 yards to the hole. I reached for a 19-degree Raylor and hit a shot that never left the pin.

The green was elevated and I couldn't see the ball land. But the gallery, which probably included 10 marshals, saw it all. The ball bounced once and rolled into the hole. It was the first double eagle in a PGA Championship since medal play began in 1958 and the fourth ever in a U.S. professional major. In fact, PGA records can't disprove that it wasn't the first since the PGA Championship began in 1916.

It was my first "albatross" – a real rare bird in golf – and I was momentarily stunned. I was trying to figure out how many under-par it was worth.

Meanwhile, network cameras had been shut down for the day, and someone asked if we had a video camera to reproduce the moment. You can imagine the look I got from my wife after I saw her in the gallery. If I had just kept quiet and let her keep the camera running.

Well, I have had many great things happen in my golf career, and there was enough film in the camera and the batteries were working as I came down the final hole of the 1996 PGA Club Professional Championship at the Arnold Palmer Private Course in La Quinta, Calif.

I was frustrated that week with my putting and I decided to change my putting grip from a normal grip to a cross-handed style.

I had never tried this before and I realized I was taking a risk trying it in competition. I finished the week with rounds of 64, 67 and 67 for a 17-under-par 271 total and broke the 28-year-old scoring record. I made a 40-foot birdie putt on the 72nd green which proved to be enough cushion to win by one stroke.

The camera picked me up raising the putter as the ball went in the hole. I got to see that ball disappear.

I never thought about the coincidence of my putting so well on a course named after "The King," but I guess it's just Fate. I have tried to keep that putting stroke, Arnie. And, we learned to keep the video camera battery charged, hoping for the sighting of more rare birds.

Darrell Kestner
Head Professional
Deepdale Golf Club
Manhasset, N.Y.

A Caddie's Tale of Glory

I'm like most PGA Members – I got into the business because I love the game. After moving to Florida in 1978 I had pretty much done it all in order to play; I had mowed greens, worked as a locker room attendant, run a bag room, become an assistant professional and done quite a bit of teaching. What happened Dec. 6-11, 1988, though, was a first for me.

I was living in West Palm Beach and was between jobs. The Chrysler Team Championship was being conducted at Palm Beach Polo in Wellington, less than 10 miles from my home. I thought it would be fun to head over to the course and try to pick up a Tour professional's bag for the week. I arrived at the main clubhouse Monday morning at 6:30 a.m. and was surprised to find that I was the first caddie on site. I had never caddied in a Tour event before, but given my extensive background in golf I was hopeful I would get a good bag.

Over the next four hours only four or five Tour professionals walked past. Meanwhile, more than 150 caddies had shown up. By 12:30 p.m. my hopes of carrying a Tour professional's bag had pretty much faded. I figured I would end up with a 23-handicap amateur in the pro-am and that would be it.

I decided to change my position and moved toward the parking lot. As I did so I recognized George Burns getting out of a gold Mercedes.

He walked up to the caddie master to see if one of his regulars had checked in. Fortunately, they had not. As he walked back to the car I asked him how he was doing and if he had anyone on the bag? He said, "No," and waved me over. I had a player! And, what a player!

We drove to one of the three courses the event would be contested on to play a practice round with Wayne Levi, his partner for the event, and Jerry Pate.

Pat Eggeling, a PGA Professional from the Metropolitan Section, was caddying for Wayne. I was having a blast. Wayne and George played solidly the first two rounds, but struggled the third day and just made the cut.

The final round, though, was magic. Both Wayne and George were hitting it close on the front nine and putts were falling. Things really got interesting on the par-5, 10th when George hit a 2-iron second shot three feet from the hole. He tapped that in and birdied the next two holes. Wayne and George were now the leaders.

They had teed off so far in front of the final group that it was tough to tell how they were really doing. A couple of birdies later, we arrived at the par-5, 17th hole. Wayne hit his tee shot into the water. George hit three good shots and had a 10-footer for birdie to push the team to 13-under-par for the day. He drained it.

As we walked off the green, George said to Wayne, "It's been a long time since I've had to make a putt that really meant something. Don't leave me alone again."

Wayne listened well. He made a 15-footer on 18 that dropped in the hole on the last roll. George had posted a 30 on the back nine and the team had rallied from seven strokes back to finish with a 59 for the lead.

We hung around in the clubhouse for the next couple of hours waiting for the final groups to finish. When the last group arrived at the 18th green, only one team had a chance to catch us – defending champions Bob Tway and Mike Hulbert. Mike was faced with a 35-footer over two hills.

Pat and I were watching on a big screen in the members bar area, high-fiving and repeating, "No way! No way that he will make this!"

Hulbert wasn't listening. He knocked the putt in the middle of the hole.

In almost total disbelief we rushed out of the bar area to prepare for the sudden death playoff. We all got into a Chrysler with a Tour official and rode to the 16th tee.

ESPN was there to capture all the action. In an amazing display of ability, Wayne slammed a 38-footer into the back of the cup … but the ball popped up as though it wasn't meant to be. Then it dropped back into the hole for the winning birdie.

I had as much fun as a first-time caddie could have. I'm happily employed now, busy at Walpole Country Club, where I have been for over a decade. I haven't caddied since, which makes me believe I may be the only undefeated caddie in the history of the Tour.

Tom Giffin
Head Professional
Walpole (Mass.) Country Club

Fan Appreciation

Last year, a few of my friends attended the Michelob Championship, in Kingsmill, Va. One of the men brought his 12-year-old son. My friends wandered around the tournament while the 12-year-old decided to follow his favorite professional, Jim Furyk. The boy followed Furyk for all 18 holes. Furyk noticed that the boy was following him and to show his appreciation for the boy's support, he took him into the golf shop after his round and bought the boy a club. Jim Furyk became an even bigger hero that day and made an unbelievable impression on a young boy … but, that is why he is a professional!

Frank Driscoll
Toano, Va.

Paul Runyan, nicknamed "Little Poison," accepts the Wanamaker Trophy in 1938 after capturing his second PGA Championship.

A Star Was Calling Me

Beginning in 1955, I would spend the next 16 years as the head professional at La Jolla (Calif.) Country Club. During that time, one of my students was a club member whom I believe was one of the best woman players to have walked the Earth.

There hasn't been a more brilliant woman player than Mickey Wright, and her record over the years, including 82 career victories, has remained a remarkable achievement.

Mickey and I were very close. I had seen her progress for about five years when I got a telephone call on a Monday. It was Mickey and she must have been about 23 years old then. She reported that she was playing in a tournament in Ohio, and that she was having trouble with her putting. She asked if I would be available and told me she was ready to fly home.

"You don't have the time to come home, your first round is Thursday," I said. "I'll give you a lesson over the phone."

As it turned out, my suggestion wasn't that major. It wasn't a big change but whatever advice she received from me that day worked perfectly. About two weeks later, Mickey won the U.S. Women's Open. With that victory and the LPGA Championship she earned earlier that season, she became the first LPGA player to win both in the same year.

Teaching the game isn't something that comes to you naturally. I was fortunate to have had several professionals who helped me. I learned much from James Norton in Hot Springs, Ark., and from two players I had helped, but who ended up teaching me as well –

Horton Smith and Macdonald Smith. Horton was a stoic and disciplined individual – he didn't need a special training program because his lifestyle was a study in training.

I think what Horton helped me transfer to my students was the knowledge of how to play the game, not to focus on techniques. He also helped me understand how to practice. Later in life I remembered Vince Lombardi's quote, "Practice does not make perfect … only perfect practice makes perfect."

When you consider I wasn't a long hitter off the tee, you'll realize I had to learn much about the whole game to survive.

I still enjoy giving lessons and folks still give me a call, asking if I'm available.

Paul Runyan
Winner of Two Major Championships
Palm Desert, Calif.

An Invaluable Lesson

In 1985, while playing golf with a member of Royal Oaks Country Club in Dallas, I suffered a great degree of pain in a span of 48 hours.

As we played the 14th hole, I attempted to make a recovery out to the fairway. Using an 8-iron, I swung and the ball caromed off the tree and hit me in the head, knocking me out cold. Two days later, playing with the same member, we reached the 15th hole and I again was faced with the same type recovery shot. I decided I would use a 7-iron this time, but changed my mind, went back to my bag and picked the same 8-iron. I swung and the ball ricocheted off another tree and hit me again. This time, I wasn't out for the count – but it really hurt! You'd think I would have learned.

That painful, but now laughable, series of events reminds of a lesson I learned while playing in a junior golf tournament while very young at Andrews Country Club in Andrews, Texas. I was 13 years old and had a miserable day on the course. Following the round, I told my playing partner to put down a par-4 for me instead of the double bogey-6 I made on the final hole. At the time I really didn't think it would matter to anyone.

As the scores went up on the board, I saw my playing partner look at the board and then give me a look that made me feel uneasy. I started to feel awful.

I got into the car with my dad for a 45-minute ride to my house. It was the worse night of my life. I couldn't wait to return the next morning to the course to clear up the situation and disqualify myself from the tournament.

I immediately went to the golf shop to find the head professional, S.A. Smith (no relation to me). I told him what happened and that I would disqualify myself.

He paused for a moment and looked at me, a young kid who had clearly not had any sleep the night before. "I see this differently," he said. "I think you have paid for your actions in the last 20 hours or so and I believe you have learned something from it. The look on your face tells me everything I need to know. You will play this next round and you're due on the tee in 10 minutes."

I finished the tournament with a 71 and I went home feeling better about myself and about the game of golf.

That PGA Professional, one of several who helped shape my career, provided me with a lesson in character and integrity that I have utilized my entire life and I go out of my way to apply to the many kids that I meet at my club.

Nobody is proud to have admitted that they have broken one of the most basic Rules of Golf, but we can feel better understanding that those same rules apply in life.

That experience as a young boy was like a good bump on the head. It was the most welcomed bump I could have ever had.

Randy Smith
Head Professional
Royal Oaks Country Club
Dallas, Texas

An Arduous Detour to the Tee

In 1996 I was the head golf professional at Mount Odin Golf Club, a municipal golf course owned by the city of Greenburg. In July, I planned to take four junior members to the pro-4 junior held at Oak Tree Country Club in West Middlesex, Pa. My car at the time was not big enough to transport all the juniors and five sets of clubs, so I borrowed the car of my city administrator. The car was an old un-marked police car that the city had retired earlier the same year.

The morning of the tournament I picked up the car, and the four youth, and we proceeded on our way to West Middlesex. We were about 45 minutes into our trip when I noticed smoke coming from the back of the car. A few seconds later, as the engine exploded, the car came to a screeching halt. The kids all sat in silence as the car began to fill with smoke and I hurried out of the car urging the kids to do the same. However, being an old police cruiser, the car doors would not open from the inside. I hurried to open the back doors and the youth rushed out. We all stood in amazement on the side of the road as the car smoked as if it was going to blow. When the engine cooled the smoke began to slow and I grabbed the keys from the ignition, popped the trunk, and four determined sandal-clad young men and myself, all carrying our golf bags, began to hitchhike the last mile to the Monroeville exit of the Pennsylvania Turnpike. From there, I phoned my brother, also a golf professional, and informed him of our circumstances. As no one had been hurt, he found the odd situation amusing and chuckled as he agreed to pick us up at the exit. We arrived at the Oak Tree Country Club a few minutes before our tee time. The kids were shaken and I had no idea how they, or myself, would play.

As we walked off the 18th green four hours later I realized that the "excitement" of the car experience had taken their minds off the pressure of the tournament and had very much calmed their nerves.

We not only had a great story to tell, but we won the event by two shots.

John Klinchock
PGA Professional
Ligonier (Pa.) Country Club

Evel's Clothes Habit

In the early 1970s, I was the winter assistant golf professional to Bob Klewin at Tucson National Golf Club in Tucson, Ariz. In those days the club hosted the "Dean Martin Tucson Open" on the PGA Tour. Due to Mr. Martin's ties to NBC, the Wednesday pro-am featured many celebrities from the entertainment world.

The day of the tournament was extremely warm; the temperature was in the 80s by mid-morning. When the door opened about 10:30 a.m., I was alone in the golf shop. The tall man, dressed in a long sleeved Western shirt, denim pants, and cowboy boots with spikes, identified himself as Evel Kneivel (Mr. Kneivel is the world famous stuntman and daredevil. He had attempted to jump the Snake River Canyon on his motorcycle the summer before).

He said the clothes he was wearing were too warm to play golf in and asked if I could help him. I told him we had a large inventory of lightweight shirts and slacks and proceeded to assist him. When he came out of the dressing room he was wearing a logoed shirt and a pair of cotton slacks. He said he liked them and asked if I could hem the slacks for him (this was the early '70s and slacks were not pre-hemmed nor did golf shops have stitching machines). When I said I would have to take them to a tailor, he indicated he could not wait. His tee time was in 30 minutes, so he asked me, "Do you have any scissors?"

I cut off the bottom of his slacks as neatly as I could and then he told me he really liked the golf shirt I gave him. He wondered if we had more in other colors. I told him we had them in 12 colors. He asked that I put aside a dozen shirts and someone would come in later to pay for everything.

The day went well and we were very busy. All the fans and spectators had departed by 4:30 p.m., darkness was near and I was alone again in the golf shop. As I was preparing to close I noticed the box of shirts for Mr. Kneivel was still there. At that same moment the door opened and a very attractive woman walked in. She said, "I am Mrs. Kneivel and I am here to pay for the shirt and slacks my husband bought." I told her that he had liked the shirt so much that he had bought another dozen. With an exasperated look she said, "Again!" and handed me a credit card embossed with "Evel Kneivel."

Being a PGA Professional is a lot of hard work. However, it's fun to interact with famous people and meeting Evel and his wife will always be a fond memory.

Harvey Ott
PGA Professional
Northmoor Country Club
Highland Park, Ill.

A Life Lesson

When my son, Andrew, was eight years old, I agreed to let him play golf with me, on a real course. I signed us up for a father and son tournament at our local course. This was only the second time he had ever played, but since he had practiced for many years his expectations were very high. However, after six holes he had made some mistakes, was very frustrated, and was in tears.

I took him aside and explained golf was like life. You think you're doing everything right and trying your best but it does not always turn out the way you plan. I told him to succeed in golf and in life, you have to forget about the last shot and go for the next one. On the way to the seventh hole, he dried his tears, and said he thought he understood. He asked me to check his alignment. It was a par-3, 117 yards. He calmed down, took a deep breath and he hit the most beautiful shot I have ever seen ... it went directly into the hole for an ace.

I shouted for joy and for the timing of an important life lesson. Our PGA Professional happened to be on the tee at the time and he made Andrew's experience even better. He said, "I have been playing for 35 years ... and you have one more hole-in-one than I do!" By the time our round was finished, the professional had told everyone in the tournament. It was like walking up to the 18th at Augusta. All the players were cheering and shaking Andrew's hand. He was presented a certificate of achievement as well as some clubhouse goodies as a reward. As great as a hole-in-one can be, our PGA Professional made it better. Andrew now knows that golf, as well as life, has its ups and downs. He is also certain of what he wants to be when he grows up ... a PGA Professional.

James Lowes
Mission Viejo, Calif.

Welcome to Golf

I was in a junior tournament at Lewistown Country Club. On the par-4 first hole, I hit a drive into the rough. I still had about 125 yards to the hole. So I decided to hit a light 8-iron just hoping to get it close. But I didn't get it close … it went directly into the hole! It was the first eagle of my life and I was jumping around screaming, "I got an eagle!" My partners stared at me with a little envy and a little amazement. I waited for them to finish the hole and, of course, I had the honor of hitting first on the next tee. There was a group in front of us, so I had time for a few practice swings. I was now really psyched and envisioned hitting my next drive 300 yards straight up the middle of the fairway. After they were out of reach, I prepared to kill it. And then – Chunk! – the ball that gave me my eagle hooked right out of bounds. Gone! I got a 9 on that hole. I spoke to my professional about what had happened and he told me, "Welcome to golf!" He gave me a lesson in how to calm down before every shot, which has served me well throughout all the years I've been playing.

Allan Bobb
Lewistown, Pa.

Golf Fundamentals Help a Booklegger

Ben Hogan's *Five Lessons: The Modern Fundamentals of Golf* was an inspirational best-seller to millions of amateur golfers upon its release in 1957. No matter what your handicap, you admired Hogan for his craftsmanship on the course and his outstanding explanation of the components of the golf swing.

Hogan's book also was a reason why I have been dedicated to spreading the word of golf and its great teachers to players everywhere. In January 1974, I founded The Booklegger and began a career path that allowed me to meet the best teachers in the game.

I wrote to Ben Hogan, congratulating him on his book and letting him know that we had been selling it to everyone in as many venues as we could. He wrote back and sent an autographed copy.

His gesture elevated my enthusiasm to seek out PGA Professionals, the heart and soul of the game. Like Ben Hogan, they have a story that is inspirational. My work was dedicated to the belief that they needed a means to bring their message to the world.

The business allowed me to meet my wife, Susan, and together we built a company that would introduce us to such renowned professionals as David Leadbetter, Jim McLean and Butch Harmon. All are bona fide teachers, creative and extremely popular with both amateurs and professionals worldwide.

Several PGA Professionals had suggested that The Booklegger exhibit at the former PGA International Golf Show in Southern California. My first booth was in an underground parking lot.

Today, we have a busy booth at the PGA Merchandise Show, a global industry forum that gathers in late January in Orlando, Fla.

When *Harvey Penick's Little Red Book* was released in 1992, I had difficulty keeping them in stock. Harvey's simple message was a boon to golfers everywhere. Harvey united us all to make the most of our days in the game. We were enchanted by Harvey's words and would learn much about the game as had his prized pupils, Ben Crenshaw and Tom Kite.

We believe that through the influence of PGA Professionals, we have been able to help them extend their expertise beyond the practice tee. We've grown along with the PGA Professional, too. My son, Robert, is taking over the administrative duties of the largest company of its kind in the world. Our team is now 20, and The PGA of America has grown past 26,000 men and women professionals.

We greatly appreciate the support The PGA of America has given us over the past quarter century. We are proud to have helped make a contribution to a wonderful game.

Guthrie Kraut
Founder
The Booklegger
Grass Valley, Calif.

Mystery Member

I served as the assistant golf professional at Sycamore Hills Golf Club in Fort Wayne, Ind., a Jack Nicklaus signature design facility that is surrounded by a rather affluent residential community.

We had some beautiful homes around the course and as you might expect, several windows were broken each season from errant golf shots. The club policy on broken windows was very simple; it was between the person who hit the shot and the homeowner. If the golfer did not 'fess up to it, then the individual who owned the home had to take care of it through their homeowner's insurance coverage. Needless to say, many of our members lived on the golf course and, policy or not, we would always make an attempt to help them locate the golfer when a window was broken due to an errant shot.

One day, I received a phone call in the golf shop from a member who explained to me that she and her family had been out of town for a few days and had come home to a broken upstairs bedroom window. I told her of our policy that we were not in any way responsible for this and she completely understood. She then went on to tell me that she had found the golf ball and that there was a personalization on the golf ball that should make it quite easy to locate the golfer. She asked if I would help by identifying the player through the use of his initials listed on the ball. She would then call the person and handle it from there. She had the incident narrowed down to the two previous days and she knew that we kept very accurate records of every player on the golf course. With that in mind, she asked me to get out our starting sheets and see if any player on the tee sheet had the initials that were imprinted on the golf ball that she had found. This was the least we could do from a service standpoint to help her out, so I went back into the office, found the starting sheets and returned to the phone.

When I got back on the phone, I asked her, "What are the initials on the ball?" She replied, "DDH II." I tried, but I could not hold in the laughter. Once I explained to her that "DDH II" was actually the model of the Dunlop ball, she got a good laugh out of it, too.

Scott Alexander
Head Professional
Zollner Golf Course
Tri-State University
Angola, Ind.